Manifest and Receive

Bridge Neuroscience, Energy, and Daily Rituals to Finally Manifest the Life You Desire

Truth Haven Publishing

Copyright © 2025 Truth Haven Publishing
All rights reserved.

No part of this publication may be reproduced, stored in a retrieval system, or transmitted in any form or by any means—electronic, mechanical, photocopying, recording, or otherwise—without the prior written permission of the author or publisher. All rights reserved under international and Pan-American copyright conventions.

Legal Notice: This publication is intended for personal use only. You may not modify, distribute, sell, use, quote, or paraphrase any part of this book without explicit consent from the author or publisher.

Disclaimer: The information contained within this book is provided for educational and entertainment purposes only. The author and publisher have made every effort to ensure the accuracy and completeness of the information presented. However, no warranties of any kind are expressed or implied. This book does not constitute legal, financial, medical, or professional advice. Readers should consult qualified professionals before applying any of the information contained herein. By reading this book, the reader agrees that the author and publisher shall not be held liable for any damages, losses, or liabilities caused directly or indirectly by the use or misuse of the information contained in this book, including but not limited to errors, omissions, or inaccuracies.

This is not the beginning of your journey. This is the moment you finally arrive

Table of Contents

Introduction: Why Manifestation Hasn't Worked (Yet) 7

Part I. Foundations 18
    Chapter 1 – The Missing Foundation 20
    Chapter 2: The Energy of Receiving 30
    Chapter 3: Reprogramming the Subconscious 42

Part II. Core Techniques 52
    Chapter 4: Visualization that Actually Works 54
    Chapter 5: The Art of Scripting 64
    Chapter 6: Emotional Alignment in Real Life 73

Part III. Integration 83
    Chapter 7 – Taking Inspired Action 84
    Chapter 8: Receiving Without Resistance 94
    Chapter 9: Building Daily Manifestation Rituals 103

Part IV. Application & Expansion 112
    Chapter 10: Manifesting Across Life Areas 113
    Chapter 11: Overcoming Setbacks and Plateaus 122
    Chapter 12: Living as the Receiver 131

Conclusion: The New Way Forward 140

Introduction: Why Manifestation Hasn't Worked (Yet)

The Hidden Gaps in Mainstream Manifestation Advice

If you've explored manifestation before, you've probably heard the same instructions repeated in countless books, videos, and social media clips: visualize your dream life, think positive thoughts, act as if what you want is already yours. These ideas can feel exciting at first. They offer hope that changing your mindset can change your reality. Yet for many people, despite diligently following this advice, little actually changes. They visualize daily, write affirmations, and repeat mantras, but their lives stay more or less the same. This disconnect is rarely addressed in mainstream manifestation teachings, and it leaves people wondering what they are doing wrong.

The truth is, most popular manifestation advice oversimplifies how our minds and bodies actually work. It focuses heavily on surface-level thinking and overlooks the deeper systems that drive behavior, perception, and energy. In other words, it encourages you to paint over a wall without repairing the cracks underneath. To understand why manifestation often feels hit or miss, we need to look closely at the missing pieces that mainstream advice tends to ignore.

Gap 1: Ignoring the Subconscious Mind

Mainstream teachings often emphasize conscious thoughts, like repeating "I am wealthy" or visualizing your dream house. While helpful, these techniques don't address the powerful influence of the subconscious mind. Research in psychology shows that as much as 90 to 95 percent of our behavior is driven by subconscious programming — beliefs and patterns formed in early life that operate automatically. If your subconscious holds the belief that money is unsafe or love always leads to pain, no amount of positive thinking will override that programming unless you intentionally rewire it. This is one of the biggest reasons people feel like they are "doing everything right" but not seeing results. They are working on the surface, while the deeper operating system runs a different script.

Gap 2: Lack of Emotional Alignment

Another common gap is the overemphasis on thoughts while neglecting emotions. Mainstream advice often implies that thinking about what you want is enough, but neuroscience and behavioral studies show otherwise. Emotions are what imprint experiences in the brain and send powerful physiological signals to the body. They are the bridge between thought and reality. If you visualize abundance but feel anxious, doubtful, or resentful inside, the energy you project is mixed. This misalignment confuses the brain and weakens your ability to stay consistent. True manifestation requires emotional coherence, where your thoughts and feelings work in harmony rather than conflict.

Gap 3: Overlooking the Role of Action

A third gap is the belief that manifestation happens purely through mental focus, with little mention of action. Many people interpret "let the universe deliver" as "do nothing and wait." This leads to passivity and missed opportunities. While manifestation is not about forcing or hustling, it does involve recognizing and acting on inspired opportunities. Mainstream teachings often fail to clarify this nuance. Without action, even the clearest vision remains an idea instead of a lived experience.

Why These Gaps Matter

These gaps are not minor details; they are the very reasons people lose faith in manifestation. When advice fails to address subconscious blocks, emotional alignment, and action, individuals blame themselves for "not manifesting correctly," which reinforces feelings of inadequacy. This cycle leaves them more disconnected from the very energy they are trying to cultivate.

In the chapters ahead, we will bridge these gaps by blending spiritual principles with practical tools and research-backed methods. But first, we need to explore how and why the overly simplistic approach became so dominant in popular culture, and why millions of people keep repeating strategies that rarely deliver consistent results.

Much of this oversimplification traces back to how manifestation ideas were popularized in modern media. When books and films condensed centuries of spiritual wisdom into catchy slogans like "ask, believe, receive," they made the concepts easy to share but stripped away crucial layers of depth. The subtle practices of self-awareness, emotional mastery, and subconscious rewiring were replaced with quick tips and blanket affirmations. This shift made manifestation appear effortless and instantly gratifying, which is appealing to audiences craving fast solutions, but it also set unrealistic expectations. People were promised life-changing results with minimal effort, and when those results didn't appear, they assumed manifestation was either a hoax or something they personally failed at.

Another reason this shallow version became dominant is its compatibility with consumer culture. Messages like "just think positive and it will happen" are easy to market and require little follow-up support. Complex teachings about inner work or emotional processing, on the other hand, are harder to distill into quick soundbites. Yet those are the very components that make manifestation truly effective. Without them, the practice is incomplete.

The cost of these gaps extends beyond disappointment. When people repeatedly attempt simplified manifestation methods and fail, they often internalize the failure as a reflection of their worth. Instead of questioning the advice, they question themselves. Thoughts like "I must not be spiritual enough" or "I don't deserve this" begin to take root. Ironically, these very beliefs deepen the subconscious blocks that prevent results. This cycle can leave someone feeling more disempowered than when they started, reinforcing the sense that life is out of their control.

Bridging these gaps requires moving beyond the idea that manifestation is purely about thinking. It involves engaging the whole person — mind, body, and emotions — and recognizing that internal alignment is as critical as the vision itself. It also requires acknowledging that manifestation is not passive. Opportunities often emerge in subtle ways, and if you are not prepared to act on them, they pass unnoticed. True manifestation blends intention with readiness, vision with response.

Practical application begins with honest self-examination. Instead of simply repeating affirmations, ask whether your underlying beliefs support or contradict what you are affirming. Notice the emotional signals in your body — tension, excitement, resistance — as they reveal whether you are aligned or conflicted. Pay attention to the actions you take each day. Are they moving you closer to the life you say you want, or reinforcing the patterns you are trying to change? These small checkpoints help close the gaps mainstream teachings ignore.

As this book unfolds, you will see that manifestation is neither mystical luck nor blind effort. It is a structured process that combines clarity of desire, emotional coherence, subconscious rewiring, and aligned action. These elements, when practiced together, create a synergy that transforms both your inner state and your external reality. Rather than chasing scattered tips, you will build a framework that integrates seamlessly into your daily life.

The coming chapters will guide you through this process step by step, grounding each practice in both practical wisdom and research that shows why it works. Understanding these hidden gaps is the first step toward closing them, and closing them is what allows manifestation to finally shift from theory into lived experience.

Why "Positive Thinking" Alone Fails to Create Results

For many people, the first piece of manifestation advice they ever hear is to "just think positive." It is simple, appealing, and easy to repeat. The concept implies that by maintaining happy thoughts, good things will naturally flow into your life. While positivity can absolutely influence your outlook and improve your emotional well-being, relying on it as the sole driver of manifestation is one of the most common reasons people do not see results. It creates the illusion that mindset alone is enough, when in reality, manifestation requires deeper alignment between your beliefs, emotions, and actions.

Positive thinking can help shift your focus away from fear and limitation, but if it is practiced in isolation, it often leads to frustration. This happens because thoughts are only one layer of the human experience. Beneath your conscious thoughts lies a vast network of subconscious programming, emotional patterns, and physiological responses that shape how you interpret reality and make decisions. These deeper layers do not automatically change just because you are repeating optimistic statements in your head. Without addressing them, positivity becomes a thin layer of paint over an unsteady foundation.

The Role of the Subconscious in Blocking Results

Studies in cognitive neuroscience reveal that most of our daily behavior is guided by subconscious processes rather than conscious thought. Dr. Joseph LeDoux's work at New York University demonstrated that emotional responses often originate in the brain before we even become aware of them. This means you can tell yourself "I am confident" all day long, but if your subconscious still associates risk with danger or failure, your body will react with stress signals like tension or avoidance. These hidden reactions can sabotage your ability to take the aligned actions needed for manifestation, even while you are consciously trying to stay positive.

This disconnect explains why affirmations sometimes feel hollow or even uncomfortable. When there is a large gap between what you are saying and what you truly believe, your mind resists the new statement. Instead of feeling inspired, you may feel like you are lying to yourself, which increases internal friction. Until those subconscious beliefs are examined and reshaped, positive thinking remains a surface-level tool rather than a transformative practice.

Emotions Carry More Weight Than Words

Another limitation of pure positive thinking is that it focuses on thoughts while ignoring emotions. Neuroscience shows that emotions carry a stronger physiological imprint than mere words. They influence heart rate, hormone release, and memory formation, signaling to the body whether an experience is safe, rewarding, or threatening. If you are saying "I am abundant" but feeling anxious about overdue bills, your emotional state will dominate your energetic signal. The result is misalignment: your mind is projecting one message, but your nervous system is broadcasting another.

This emotional mismatch also affects perception. The brain's reticular activating system filters information based on what feels most relevant or emotionally charged. When fear or doubt is stronger than hope, you unconsciously focus on evidence that supports fear rather than possibilities that align with your desires. Simply layering positive thoughts on top does not rewrite these deeper filters.

Why Action Cannot Be Ignored

The final problem with relying solely on positive thinking is that it often leads to passivity. Many people interpret manifestation advice to mean that if they just think happy thoughts, the universe will do the rest. But manifestation is not about bypassing effort; it is about aligning effort with intention. Opportunities arise frequently, yet they are only life-changing if you recognize and act on them. Positive thinking can set the stage, but without inspired action, it rarely leads to tangible results.

Understanding these limits of positivity sets the foundation for a more complete manifestation practice. The next step is to explore how thoughts can still play a powerful role when combined with emotion, belief work, and aligned behaviors.

When positive thinking is reframed as one part of a larger process, it becomes far more effective. Optimistic thoughts help direct your attention toward what you want, but their real power emerges when they are integrated with emotional coherence and deeper belief work. Instead of forcing yourself to repeat statements that feel untrue, the focus shifts toward creating thoughts that your body and subconscious can accept and expand upon. This begins by recognizing that thoughts are signals, not magic spells. They inform the nervous system of where to focus, but they must be supported by internal alignment to create lasting change.

Research on neuroplasticity supports this approach. Dr. Richard Davidson's studies at the University of Wisconsin showed that sustained positive emotions and thoughts physically alter the brain's circuitry related to resilience and well-being. However, the changes occurred not just from thinking happy thoughts but from cultivating practices, like meditation and emotional regulation, that consistently reinforced them. This illustrates that repetition alone is not enough; the brain responds to consistency paired with genuine emotional experience.

To create this alignment, it helps to bridge the gap between current reality and desired reality gradually. Rather than jumping from "I am broke" to "I am a millionaire," which may trigger inner resistance, you can adopt bridging thoughts that feel believable, such as "I am learning to create more stability with money" or "I am open to new ways of increasing my income." These thoughts still point toward your goal but reduce the internal conflict that pure positive affirmations often provoke. Over time, as evidence builds and beliefs shift, stronger affirmations become natural rather than forced.

Another essential element is taking feedback from your emotional state seriously. Instead of ignoring doubt or pushing it away with more positivity, use it as information. Doubt often reveals where subconscious beliefs are misaligned or where practical steps are missing. By addressing these directly — through tools like journaling, visualization, or guided belief work — you transform doubt into a guide rather than an obstacle.

Positive thinking also becomes more potent when paired with action that confirms the new identity you are building. Identity-based habits are powerful because they signal to your subconscious that change is already underway. For example, if you are working on abundance, taking small but consistent actions to manage your finances or explore new income opportunities reinforces the belief that you are capable and proactive. This feedback loop between thought, emotion, and behavior strengthens the manifestation process far beyond what isolated optimism can achieve.

The most important shift is understanding that manifestation is not about pretending problems do not exist. It is about approaching them from a state of clarity and possibility rather than fear and resignation. Positive thinking, when used in this integrated way, helps maintain hope and vision, but it is grounded in practical steps and emotional honesty. This balance is what allows you to sustain momentum without burning out or falling into self-blame when challenges arise.

By moving beyond simplistic positivity, you open the door to a manifestation practice that feels authentic, rooted in both science and spirit, and capable of producing real results. In the next section, we will look at how this integrated approach forms the core framework of the book, combining clarity of desire, subconscious reprogramming, emotional alignment, and inspired action into a cohesive path you can follow daily.

How This Book Will Finally Bridge Science, Energy, and Daily Life for You

Most people who explore manifestation find themselves caught between two extremes. On one side is the purely spiritual perspective that speaks about energy, vibration, and the universe responding to intention. On the other side is the purely practical advice rooted in productivity, habits, and goal-setting. Each approach offers valuable insights, but when taken alone, they often feel incomplete. The spiritual side can seem abstract and ungrounded, while the practical side can feel mechanical and disconnected from deeper meaning. What is rarely offered is a framework that integrates both: a process that honors the unseen energetic forces shaping our reality and the tangible steps required to anchor them into daily life.

This book was written to fill that gap. Its purpose is to show you not only *what* to do but *why* it works, supported by research from neuroscience, psychology, and behavioral science. At the same time, it acknowledges the intuitive and spiritual dimensions of manifestation that have been practiced for centuries. This union of science and energy creates a practical pathway you can follow without feeling like you are choosing between two conflicting worlds.

Why Science Matters in Manifestation

Many manifestation teachings ask you to take ideas on faith alone, which can feel frustrating if you are someone who craves understanding. When results do not show up immediately, doubt creeps in, and without a clear explanation, it is easy to assume nothing is happening. By grounding manifestation practices in research, this book removes that uncertainty. For example, studies on neuroplasticity show that the brain physically changes in response to repeated thoughts and emotional experiences. This is the very mechanism behind why visualization, affirmations, and emotional alignment work: they are not just abstract rituals but exercises that reshape neural pathways over time.

Consider the research of Dr. Richard Davidson at the University of Wisconsin, which revealed that sustained positive emotional states correlate with structural changes in the brain regions linked to resilience and well-being. His findings confirm that cultivating emotions like gratitude and joy is not just "feel good" advice; it is a biological process that influences how you perceive and respond to life events. By including insights like these, this book allows you to see your practices as more than wishful thinking. You will understand the changes happening inside your mind and body, which makes it easier to stay consistent and trust the process.

Why Energy Still Matters

While science explains *how* practices work, it cannot fully capture the lived experience of connecting with something larger than yourself. Manifestation involves more than rewiring the brain; it is about aligning with a sense of possibility, meaning, and intuition that often defies rational explanation. Energy is the bridge between thought and form, the subtle force that links your inner state with external outcomes. Ignoring this dimension can make manifestation feel dry and transactional, as if it were just another productivity hack.

The energy perspective reminds you that life is not simply about controlling outcomes but about co-creating with a larger field of intelligence. Whether you view that field as the universe, God, or your own higher self, acknowledging it opens the door to deeper trust and surrender. When you combine this spiritual awareness with practical tools and evidence-based strategies, manifestation becomes both grounded and expansive — something you can practice daily without losing its sense of wonder.

The true test of any manifestation practice is not how inspiring it sounds in theory but how seamlessly it fits into your everyday life. It is one thing to feel motivated after reading a book or watching a video; it is another to consistently apply what you learn during a stressful workday, when doubts surface, or when external circumstances seem unchanged. This is where most approaches fail: they provide lofty ideas but little guidance on turning them into sustainable habits. The framework you are about to explore has been designed to address this exact problem, breaking concepts into actionable steps without losing sight of the deeper principles behind them.

Daily integration begins with awareness. Instead of waiting for perfect conditions or large amounts of free time, you will learn how to weave manifestation into the small spaces of your day — morning routines, transitions between tasks, moments of reflection before bed. This does not require hours of meditation or elaborate rituals. It requires intentional focus, an understanding of which practices move the needle, and consistency that builds over time. By structuring this book around both theory and practical exercises, you will gain tools you can apply immediately and refine as you go.

This blend of science and energy also solves another common challenge: maintaining belief when progress is not immediately visible. Knowing that your brain is actively forming new pathways or that your emotional state is shifting measurable physiological responses keeps you anchored during the quiet periods of growth. At the same time, honoring the energetic side of manifestation helps you remain open to unexpected opportunities and intuitive nudges that logic alone might dismiss. This combination creates a steady sense of trust rather than the anxious waiting that often accompanies purely goal-focused approaches.

Throughout the chapters ahead, you will encounter specific practices — visualization methods rooted in neuroscience, scripting techniques supported by studies on narrative psychology, gratitude rituals shown to increase well-being, and strategies for identifying and reprogramming subconscious blocks. Each will be explained clearly, with guidance on how to adapt them to your unique circumstances. This flexibility is crucial because manifestation is not one-size-fits-all. Your experiences, beliefs, and goals are distinct, which means the path to alignment must be personalized rather than rigid.

You will also see how these practices intersect. Visualization alone can be powerful, but when paired with emotional regulation and aligned action, it becomes exponentially more effective. Gratitude not only elevates your mood but primes your brain to notice opportunities you might otherwise overlook. Scripting clarifies your desires, while small daily actions confirm them to your subconscious. Each element reinforces the others, creating momentum that builds naturally rather than forcing results.

By the end of this book, the aim is for manifestation to feel less like a separate activity and more like a way of living. You will not need to constantly check whether it is "working," because you will understand the inner shifts taking place and how they lead to external change. This knowledge removes the guesswork and brings manifestation out of the realm of wishful thinking into something tangible, repeatable, and deeply empowering.

Part I. Foundations

Before you learn the techniques that make manifestation work, you need to build the ground beneath them. Without a stable foundation, even the most inspiring tools lose their power. This is the stage where you create clarity about what you want, understand the energy that drives your experiences, and begin reshaping the subconscious patterns that quietly determine so much of your reality.

Most people who struggle with manifestation never take this step seriously. They jump straight into visualizing or repeating affirmations, hoping that enthusiasm alone will carry them to their goals. At first, this rush of positivity feels motivating. But when results do not come, they assume something is wrong with them rather than realizing the real issue: their inner blueprint has not been aligned with what they are trying to create. You cannot build a house on shifting ground. Similarly, you cannot manifest a new reality while carrying unexamined beliefs, conflicting emotions, or unclear intentions.

This first part of the book exists to solve that problem. Over the next three chapters, you will move through a process of defining what you want, learning how energy and emotion shape your experiences, and uncovering the subconscious programming that may be keeping you stuck. These are not abstract ideas. They are practical skills that give structure to everything that follows. When you know what you truly want, when you can feel your energy state shifting, and when you understand the deeper patterns influencing your decisions, manifestation stops being a guessing game.

You will start by creating clarity. This means separating true desires from borrowed ones — the things you think you should want because of cultural expectations, social media comparisons, or old family narratives. Clarity is not about perfection; it is about honesty. The more precise you are about your intentions, the easier it becomes for your mind and body to organize around them.

Next, you will explore the energy of receiving. This is where you begin to recognize how your emotions broadcast signals long before words do, and how those signals quietly influence what you notice and attract.

Understanding this concept helps you stop fighting your own emotional patterns and start working with them.

Finally, you will uncover and reprogram subconscious beliefs. This step reveals why you might sabotage your goals or struggle to trust the process. Once you see these patterns clearly, you can begin to shift them, creating space for new beliefs that support the reality you are building.

By the time you finish Part I, you will have a foundation that feels solid and aligned. You will know what you are manifesting, why it matters to you, and how to start tuning your energy and beliefs toward it. From here, the techniques in later parts of the book will not just inspire you — they will work, because you will have prepared the ground for them to take root.

Chapter 1 – The Missing Foundation

Clarity vs. Chaos: Why You Can't Manifest What You Don't Define

One of the most overlooked truths in manifestation is that you cannot attract what you cannot define. Vague intentions create vague results. When your goals are unclear, your energy is scattered, and your actions lack direction. It becomes almost impossible to notice opportunities or align your behavior with what you want because you have not decided what that is in the first place. This lack of clarity is why so many people feel stuck: they are asking the universe for "a better life" or "more abundance," but they have not translated those desires into something tangible enough for their mind and emotions to organize around.

Clarity is not about locking yourself into a rigid plan or knowing every detail of how your life will unfold. It is about giving your subconscious and conscious mind a clear target. Without this, your brain struggles to filter information effectively. The human brain processes thousands of sensory inputs every second, yet it can only consciously focus on a small fraction. To manage this, it relies on a mechanism called the reticular activating system (RAS), which acts like a filter, prioritizing what aligns with your current goals or perceived needs. When your goals are undefined, this system has nothing specific to look for, which is why opportunities often go unnoticed even when they are right in front of you.

The Science Behind Clear Goals

Research in goal-setting psychology consistently shows that specific goals outperform general ones. In one landmark study by Dr. Edwin Locke and Dr. Gary Latham, individuals with clearly defined goals were significantly more likely to achieve them than those with vague aspirations. Specific goals create focus, generate motivation, and help you measure progress, which is essential for sustaining effort over time. When applied to manifestation, this means that defining exactly what you want does not limit the magic of the process — it enhances it by giving your energy direction.

Neuroscience supports this as well. When you clarify a goal, you create what psychologists call "implementation intentions," which are mental blueprints for action. These blueprints trigger the RAS to scan your environment for relevant cues, making you more likely to recognize synchronicities or opportunities you might otherwise ignore. This is not coincidence; it is your brain's natural pattern-recognition system working in your favor once it has been given a clear signal.

Chaos and Conflicting Desires

Lack of clarity does not just mean not knowing what you want. It can also mean wanting contradictory things at the same time. You might desire financial freedom but secretly fear the responsibility that comes with wealth. You might long for love while holding onto beliefs that relationships lead to pain. These conflicting desires create energetic chaos, sending mixed signals that dilute manifestation efforts. Until these contradictions are resolved, you remain stuck in a cycle of stop-and-go progress, making small gains only to self-sabotage or retreat.

This is why the first step in any effective manifestation practice is slowing down to define your desires with honesty and depth. It is not enough to want "more money" or "better health." What does more money mean to you? Is it freedom to travel, the ability to support your family, or peace of mind knowing your bills are covered? What does better health look like in your daily life — more energy to play with your kids, the confidence to move without pain, or the longevity to experience life fully? Without this level of specificity, the mind cannot build a compelling vision, and without a vision, the subconscious cannot support you in creating it.

The process of uncovering authentic desires begins with separating what is truly yours from what you have absorbed from others. Many people set goals based on cultural expectations, family pressure, or comparisons to peers rather than genuine longing. This creates a subtle sense of resistance because the vision does not resonate at a deeper level. One of the most powerful questions you can ask yourself is, "If no one else ever saw what I achieved, would I still want this?" It forces you to look beyond appearances and focus on what genuinely fulfills you.

Clarity also involves translating abstract ideas into concrete images and feelings. Instead of declaring that you want "success," explore what success actually looks like in your daily experience. How do you wake up in the morning? Where do you spend your time? What conversations are you having? The clearer you become about the sensory and emotional details, the easier it is for your subconscious to anchor to that vision. This is where visualization becomes more than daydreaming; it becomes a form of mental rehearsal that primes your nervous system for change.

Dr. Benjamin Hardy's work on future self psychology emphasizes this point. His research shows that people who regularly imagine their "future self" in vivid detail make decisions more aligned with long-term goals than those who keep their vision vague. By consistently connecting with this future identity, you begin to bridge the gap between where you are and where you are going, making choices that naturally support your desired reality.

An equally important part of gaining clarity is addressing conflicting desires directly rather than ignoring them. It is normal to want multiple things at once, but unresolved contradictions create inner friction that slows progress. For example, you may want to manifest love while fearing vulnerability, or desire more income while fearing judgment for wanting wealth. Bringing these tensions to the surface allows you to examine their roots and decide which beliefs are worth keeping and which must evolve. Without this inner honesty, even the most polished vision boards fail to generate lasting change.

Practical clarity does not mean locking yourself into a rigid outcome. It means knowing the essence of what you want so you can recognize aligned opportunities when they arise. Flexibility is key because life often delivers in ways you could not have predicted. By defining the feeling and core qualities of your desired outcome — freedom, connection, peace, creativity — you stay open to possibilities while maintaining focus. This balance allows manifestation to unfold in a way that is both intentional and organic.

As you move through the exercises in this book, you will refine your vision repeatedly. Clarity is not a one-time event but an evolving process that deepens as you learn more about yourself. With each layer of definition, your thoughts, emotions, and actions begin to organize around a single direction rather than scattering energy in conflicting paths. This unified focus creates momentum and makes the manifestation process feel less like struggle and more like alignment.

In the next chapter, you will build on this foundation by exploring how energy and emotion influence what you attract. Understanding clarity is the first step; learning to align your internal state with that clarity is what transforms possibility into reality.

How to Uncover True Desires (Not Just What You Think You Want)

One of the biggest reasons manifestation efforts fail is that people are often unclear about what they truly want at a core level. They set goals based on surface desires, societal pressure, or what they believe they should want rather than what would actually fulfill them. This creates a subtle but powerful misalignment. You might consciously chase a career title, a specific amount of money, or a particular relationship, only to realize later that achieving it does not bring the satisfaction you expected. The result is confusion and frustration, leading many to believe manifestation does not work, when in reality they were manifesting the wrong things.

True desires come from a deeper place than quick wishes or reactive goals. They are rooted in your values, your authentic needs, and the experiences that make you feel most alive. Uncovering these desires requires honest reflection and the willingness to look beyond superficial wants. This process is not about rejecting ambition or material goals; it is about making sure that whatever you pursue genuinely resonates with who you are and the life you want to create.

The Difference Between Surface and Core Desires

Surface desires often arise from comparison or temporary discomfort. For example, wanting a luxury car might be about status rather than freedom or comfort. Craving a high-paying job might stem from fear of scarcity rather than passion for the work. Core desires, by contrast, tend to reflect deeper emotional needs such as safety, love, autonomy, or creative expression. When you identify the core need driving a goal, you can manifest in ways that satisfy the underlying yearning rather than chasing endless external markers.

Research on intrinsic versus extrinsic motivation supports this distinction. Psychologists Edward Deci and Richard Ryan, through their Self-Determination Theory, demonstrated that goals aligned with intrinsic values — personal growth, connection, mastery — lead to greater satisfaction and sustained motivation than those driven by external rewards like approval or status. Applying this to manifestation means that uncovering your true desires is not just spiritually aligned but also psychologically effective in creating lasting fulfillment.

Why True Desires Are Hard to Access

Many people struggle to identify authentic desires because they are buried under layers of conditioning. From childhood, we absorb messages about what success looks like, what relationships should be, and what kind of life is "acceptable." These inherited narratives shape our default goals, often without us realizing it. Social media intensifies this by constantly showcasing curated versions of other people's lives, which can lead us to pursue goals that look impressive but feel hollow once achieved.

Another barrier is fear. Sometimes we do know what we truly want but avoid admitting it because it feels too big, too unrealistic, or too risky. Acknowledging a desire for deep intimacy, creative freedom, or radical lifestyle change can be intimidating because it forces us to confront doubts and question old beliefs about what is possible. Yet ignoring these desires does not make them disappear; it only creates an inner tension that drains energy and clarity.

Uncovering true desires is therefore an act of both honesty and courage. It requires turning inward rather than outward, listening to your intuition, and allowing yourself to imagine a life that feels deeply meaningful, even if it challenges the expectations you have carried for years.

Revealing these deeper desires begins with creating enough quiet space to hear them. In daily life, constant noise from obligations, social media, and internal chatter often drowns out intuition. Simple practices like journaling or mindful reflection help strip away these layers so you can notice what consistently calls to you. Pay attention to recurring thoughts or longings that appear even when you are not actively trying to set goals. These are often clues pointing toward your authentic path.

Another helpful method is to explore what feelings you are truly chasing behind your goals. When you picture having the relationship, career, or lifestyle you want, focus on how you imagine feeling in that reality. Is it freedom, safety, joy, or belonging? Naming the emotion underneath the desire helps you identify whether your current goals actually align with what you are seeking. Sometimes you will discover that the form of the goal can change as long as the feeling is honored.

A reflective exercise often used in coaching and therapy is the "five whys." Start with a stated goal, then ask yourself "Why do I want this?" five times in succession, answering each question honestly. The first answer might be superficial, but by the fourth or fifth, you often uncover the real motivation — a longing for connection, autonomy, or meaning. This process removes layers of conditioning and surfaces the value driving your desire.

Research on life satisfaction reinforces the value of this deeper clarity. A study by psychologist Tim Kasser on materialistic versus intrinsic goals found that people who pursued goals aligned with intrinsic values like personal growth and community experienced higher well-being, even when they faced external challenges. This suggests that choosing goals rooted in authentic desires not only supports manifestation but also improves quality of life in ways that external markers of success cannot replicate.

Once you gain clarity about your true desires, it becomes easier to let go of goals that were never truly yours. This act of release is as important as defining what you want. Holding onto inauthentic goals creates friction, consuming energy that could be directed toward intentions that genuinely inspire you. Many people find that when they release goals rooted in comparison or fear, they experience an immediate sense of relief and spaciousness, which often allows clearer opportunities to emerge.

The final step in this process is to begin trusting what you discover. It can be unsettling to realize that what you deeply want may look very different from what others expect of you, but authenticity is the foundation of sustainable manifestation. Aligning with desires that come from your core values makes it easier to stay committed when challenges arise, because you are no longer motivated by appearances or external validation. You are motivated by something far stronger: the pull of a life that feels like your own.

By uncovering true desires, you are setting the stage for manifestation to work in its most powerful way. The clarity you create here will inform the visualizations you build, the actions you take, and the beliefs you reinforce in the chapters ahead. As you move forward, you will use this authentic foundation to guide every step of the process, ensuring that what you manifest does not just arrive but genuinely fulfills you.

Designing Your Life Vision Without Overwhelm

Creating a life vision is one of the most transformative steps in manifestation, yet it is also one of the most intimidating. The idea of mapping out your ideal future can bring up excitement, but just as easily it can trigger anxiety and perfectionism. Many people delay this process because they feel they must have every detail figured out or fear committing to a vision they might later outgrow. The pressure to design the "perfect" life vision often leads to procrastination, scattered focus, or simply giving up before they start.

The purpose of a life vision is not to trap you in a rigid plan but to give you direction. Think of it like setting coordinates in a navigation system: you do not need to know every turn you will take, but you must know where you are heading. Without this sense of direction, manifestation remains unfocused. The mind cannot organize around something vague, and opportunities pass by unnoticed. With clarity, your subconscious begins filtering daily choices and external cues, allowing you to spot patterns, synchronicities, and solutions that align with your goal.

Shifting from Pressure to Possibility

One reason vision work feels overwhelming is that people approach it as a single life-defining decision rather than an evolving practice. They believe they must predict every detail of the next five or ten years, which can feel paralyzing. The truth is, your vision will grow with you. What matters now is defining the essence of what you want to create: the feelings, values, and priorities that will guide your decisions. When you allow space for evolution, designing a vision stops feeling like a test you must pass and starts feeling like a process of discovery.

It also helps to release the idea that you must choose between practicality and dreaming big. A powerful vision holds both: it inspires you while remaining grounded enough to feel believable. If your vision feels completely unattainable, your subconscious may resist it. If it feels too small, it will not ignite the energy required for transformation. The sweet spot is a vision that stretches you without overwhelming you, one that invites growth while still feeling anchored in possibility.

The Science of Visualization and Clarity

Research in cognitive psychology shows that mental imagery activates similar neural pathways to real-life experience. Studies by Dr. Guang Yue and others demonstrate that even imagining physical actions can strengthen neural circuits associated with those actions. This is why a vivid life vision has such power: it conditions your brain to expect the reality you are envisioning, making you more likely to notice and act on opportunities that align with it. When your brain has a clear picture, it works quietly in the background, priming you to take steps that feel natural rather than forced.

At the same time, neuroscience warns against overly vague visions. The reticular activating system, the brain's filtering mechanism, responds to specificity. When you define details — not just "abundance" but "financial freedom to choose where I live and how I spend my days" — your mind knows what to look for. This does not mean obsessing over every minor detail but painting a picture rich enough to evoke emotion and direct focus.

To make the visioning process feel manageable, start with the bigger picture and refine details gradually. Begin by focusing on the main areas of life that matter to you most — relationships, work, health, personal growth, and contribution. Identify the qualities you want to experience in each area rather than fixating on exact outcomes. Instead of pressuring yourself to describe every aspect of a dream job or home, clarify the feelings and values you want those environments to hold. This focus on qualities provides direction while leaving space for flexibility as your life evolves.

Clarity emerges through immersion rather than speed. Allow yourself to revisit and expand your vision over several sessions rather than trying to complete it in one sitting. The act of returning to it repeatedly signals to your subconscious that this vision matters, which deepens emotional connection and builds momentum. Some people find it helpful to write freely about an ideal day in their future life, describing what they see, hear, and feel from morning to night. Others prefer creating a visual representation through images or symbols that evoke the same emotions. Both methods work as long as they feel natural and engaging to you.

Addressing overwhelm also means recognizing and neutralizing the perfectionism that often arises during this process. There is no "wrong" way to create a life vision. The purpose is not to impress anyone or predict every twist and turn ahead. The purpose is to generate clarity and alignment so your thoughts, emotions, and actions begin moving in the same direction. Remind yourself that your vision is allowed to evolve; what you define today is simply the next chapter, not the entire story.

Research on goal-setting shows that breaking big visions into smaller milestones increases both motivation and follow-through. Psychologists Teresa Amabile and Steven Kramer discovered that recognizing even small wins releases dopamine, which boosts engagement and resilience. Translating this to manifestation, every step you take toward your vision — writing down intentions, adjusting habits, practicing gratitude — reinforces belief and reduces the sense of overwhelm that comes from focusing only on the distant end goal.

As you refine your life vision, trust the interplay between specificity and openness. Include enough detail to spark emotion and activate your brain's filtering system, but leave space for outcomes to unfold in ways you might not predict. This balance prevents rigidity and allows room for unexpected opportunities that may fit your core desires even better than what you initially imagined.

When you reach the point where your vision feels vivid and energizing, you will notice a subtle shift. Decisions become easier, distractions lose their pull, and you begin to interpret challenges differently. Rather than questioning whether you are on the right path, you start recognizing how each experience fits into the larger picture you are building. This shift is not forced; it emerges naturally as your internal state and external reality start to align.

By approaching your vision with curiosity rather than pressure, you transform what could feel like an overwhelming task into an inspiring practice. The clarity you gain here will serve as the compass for every manifestation tool you learn in the chapters ahead, ensuring that each visualization, affirmation, and action is grounded in a vision that feels undeniably yours.

Chapter 2: The Energy of Receiving

Understanding Frequency and Emotional Setpoints (No Fluff)

When people talk about "vibrations" or "frequency" in manifestation circles, the language often becomes abstract or overly mystical. This can make the concept seem unapproachable, as if it belongs to an exclusive spiritual realm rather than something practical you can understand and apply. The reality is that frequency is not a magical force separate from daily life. It is simply a way of describing the emotional and physiological states you spend most of your time in — and how those states influence your thoughts, actions, and perception of opportunities.

Every human being operates with what psychologists call a baseline or "setpoint" of emotion. This setpoint is shaped by past experiences, beliefs, and habits of thought, and it functions almost like a default emotional thermostat. Some people naturally live in a range of optimism and curiosity, while others find themselves hovering near anxiety or frustration without always knowing why. These habitual emotional states are what spiritual teachings refer to as your vibration.

The importance of emotional setpoints in manifestation is that they determine how you interpret reality. Two people can experience the same event and respond in completely different ways based on their emotional baseline. Someone whose setpoint leans toward fear might see an opportunity and immediately think of what could go wrong, while someone whose setpoint is rooted in trust might view the same opportunity as a potential breakthrough. This difference in perception influences not just how they feel but also what actions they take — and those actions ultimately shape outcomes.

The Physiology of Emotional Frequency

There is nothing mystical about emotions affecting the body. Neuroscience and psychophysiology show that emotions are closely tied to hormonal and nervous system responses. For example, chronic stress triggers cortisol release, heightening vigilance and narrowing focus toward potential threats. On the other hand, emotions like gratitude and joy stimulate neurotransmitters such as dopamine and serotonin, which broaden your awareness and increase creativity. This connection is central to manifestation because your ability to notice opportunities and make empowered choices depends on the state you are in.

Dr. Barbara Fredrickson's research on the "broaden and build" theory demonstrates that positive emotional states expand cognitive flexibility. When you feel uplifted, you are more likely to see creative solutions and recognize resources that are invisible during states of fear or frustration. This does not mean you must force yourself to feel happy all the time. It means that cultivating emotional awareness and intentionally shifting your baseline over time allows you to access states where manifestation becomes more fluid and natural.

Setpoints and Conditioning

Emotional setpoints are not fixed at birth; they develop through repeated experiences and the meanings you assign to them. If you grew up in an environment where money was always associated with stress or scarcity, your emotional setpoint around finances may lean toward anxiety, even if your current circumstances are stable. Similarly, if relationships were modeled with conflict, you might carry a subtle expectation of disappointment into new connections. These patterns often run below conscious awareness but shape how easily you trust, receive, and act.

Understanding this helps remove the blame many people feel when manifestation does not work quickly. You are not "failing" to manifest because you are flawed or unlucky. You are working with patterns that have been reinforced for years, sometimes decades. The good news is that setpoints can be shifted. Neuroplasticity — the brain's ability to rewire itself — shows that repeated new emotional experiences create new neural pathways, gradually replacing old patterns with healthier defaults.

The first step in shifting your setpoint is awareness. Most people live in their emotional patterns without noticing them, reacting to circumstances rather than observing their internal responses. Developing awareness begins with paying attention to how you feel in ordinary moments rather than only during extremes. Noticing subtle cues — tension in your body, repetitive thoughts, or habitual reactions to minor stressors — helps you recognize your current baseline. This observation is not about judgment; it is about gathering information so you can respond with intention instead of autopilot.

Once awareness is established, the next step is gently introducing new emotional experiences. Trying to leap from frustration to bliss in one jump is unrealistic and often backfires. A more effective approach is incremental — shifting from frustration to neutrality, from neutrality to curiosity, and from curiosity to genuine optimism over time. This gradual climb builds emotional resilience, which is far more sustainable than forcing yourself to stay in artificially high states.

One powerful way to support this shift is through gratitude practices. Gratitude is not simply about listing good things; it is about training the brain to notice what is already working. Studies by Dr. Robert Emmons and Dr. Michael McCullough showed that people who regularly practiced gratitude experienced higher well-being and lower levels of stress hormones compared to control groups. Over time, this focus rewires neural pathways, making it easier to access elevated emotional states without conscious effort.

Equally important is addressing triggers that consistently pull you back into lower states. If certain environments, habits, or relationships repeatedly reinforce stress or self-doubt, they deserve honest examination. This does not mean avoiding discomfort entirely but creating enough supportive structure to allow your new patterns to take root. For example, reducing exposure to constant negative news while increasing time spent in restorative environments can significantly stabilize your baseline.

Physiological regulation also plays a crucial role in shifting frequency. Breathwork, meditation, and mindful movement influence the vagus nerve, which governs the body's stress response. Simple techniques like slow, deep breathing can calm the nervous system in minutes, creating an opening to choose different thoughts and actions. Over time, these practices train your body to return to balance more quickly after stress, gradually raising your setpoint.

As your baseline begins to shift, you will notice changes in how you interpret daily events. Situations that once triggered immediate frustration may feel less threatening. Opportunities that previously went unnoticed begin to stand out. This change in perception is not coincidental; it reflects the brain's adaptive filtering system responding to your new emotional pattern. The more consistently you inhabit supportive states, the more naturally aligned your decisions and behaviors become with your desired outcomes.

Mastering your frequency is not about achieving perfection or eliminating all negative emotions. It is about creating enough emotional stability to navigate life without constantly being pulled back into old patterns. From this steadier place, manifestation becomes less about pushing for results and more about allowing them to unfold as you align your inner state with the reality you are creating.

How Thoughts and Emotions Interact to Shape Reality

Manifestation is often described as a mental process, as though thinking positively is enough to attract what you desire. But thoughts on their own are not the full story. They interact constantly with emotions, creating a feedback loop that either strengthens or weakens your ability to shape reality. Understanding this interplay is crucial because it reveals why two people can hold the same thought — "I want financial freedom," for example — yet experience entirely different results. The difference lies not just in the thought itself, but in the emotional energy attached to it.

Thoughts are the language of the mind. They frame what you focus on, what you believe is possible, and how you interpret the events around you. Emotions are the language of the body. They are felt responses that signal safety, excitement, fear, or desire. When these two align, the message you send inwardly and outwardly is coherent. When they conflict, your system becomes divided, often leading to mixed results or self-sabotage.

The Feedback Loop Between Mind and Body

Neuroscience confirms that thoughts and emotions do not operate in isolation. When you have a thought, it triggers chemical reactions in the brain that generate an emotional response. That emotion then influences subsequent thoughts, either reinforcing the original idea or spiraling it into a completely different direction. For instance, thinking about a new opportunity might generate excitement, which encourages more optimistic thoughts, building momentum toward action. Conversely, if the same thought triggers anxiety, it may cascade into doubts and avoidance.

This cycle creates what psychologists call "cognitive-emotional patterns," habitual loops that shape how you perceive and respond to life. Over time, these patterns become self-fulfilling. If your thoughts and emotions repeatedly pair scarcity with money, you are likely to interpret financial events through a lens of lack, even when opportunities are present. If you pair love with fear of loss, you may unconsciously sabotage intimacy to avoid potential pain. Recognizing these loops is the first step to rewriting them.

Why Emotion Amplifies Manifestation

Emotions give thoughts weight. A thought without emotion is like a blueprint with no energy behind it — technically complete but lacking the drive to be built. When you feel strong emotion about a thought, your body produces corresponding physiological states, signaling to the brain that this idea is significant. The reticular activating system begins filtering reality to confirm the belief, scanning for evidence that matches your emotional state. Dr. Antonio Damasio's research on decision-making shows that emotion is central to how humans prioritize information and act. People with damage to emotional processing areas of the brain struggle to make even simple choices despite having intact logic. This illustrates why manifestation rooted in thought alone often fails. Without emotional engagement, there is little motivation to act or notice opportunities, and the signal you project remains weak and inconsistent.

Harnessing this principle means pairing clear thoughts with elevated emotions. Gratitude, excitement, and curiosity are particularly effective because they expand cognitive flexibility and encourage creative problem solving. When you imagine your future with these feelings rather than fear or doubt, you prime both your conscious and subconscious mind to move toward that reality in practical ways.

Creating alignment begins with noticing when thoughts and emotions are sending different messages. A person might think, "I am capable of earning more," but feel anxious or doubtful the moment they picture taking action toward that goal. This emotional resistance signals that there is an unresolved belief or memory operating in the background. Rather than forcing positivity, it is more effective to address the source of the discomfort so that the thought and feeling can move in the same direction.

One way to do this is through emotional awareness practices. Taking a few minutes each day to check in with what you are feeling — without judgment — creates space between stimulus and reaction. Simply naming emotions, a technique supported by research from UCLA psychologist Matthew Lieberman, reduces their intensity and engages the prefrontal cortex, the part of the brain responsible for regulation and problem-solving. Once the charge of the emotion softens, it becomes easier to introduce thoughts that guide you toward balance rather than conflict.

Shifting emotions is not about suppressing what feels uncomfortable. It is about choosing thoughts that gently redirect your state without invalidating your experience. If fear arises around a financial goal, instead of jumping to "I am rich and successful," which might feel false, a bridging thought like "I am learning to handle money in new ways" can create relief and openness. This incremental shift builds coherence between the mind and body and avoids the inner resistance that comes from affirmations that feel out of reach.

Pairing thought and emotion also becomes stronger through visualization. When you imagine a desired outcome vividly, engaging multiple senses, your body responds as though it is already happening. Heart rate, breathing, and hormone responses mirror real experiences. This phenomenon, documented in numerous studies on mental rehearsal in athletes, shows why emotionally charged imagery accelerates change: it conditions the nervous system to view the outcome as familiar, lowering resistance when opportunities arise to make it real.

Gratitude practices further deepen this interaction. By focusing on something you appreciate, you prime both thought and emotion to align in a higher state. This combination of elevated feeling and intentional focus creates a neurological imprint that reinforces belief in possibility. Over time, gratitude acts as a stabilizer, preventing the pendulum swings between extreme optimism and discouragement that can derail manifestation efforts. The more often you pair constructive thoughts with supportive emotions, the stronger the neural pathways connecting them become. Neuroplasticity ensures that repetition wires these patterns into default responses. Eventually, you no longer need to force alignment; it becomes automatic. What once felt unnatural evolves into your new normal, and this shift is what allows manifestation to feel effortless rather than forced.

Mastering this interaction is less about perfection and more about consistency. Even subtle improvements in how you think and feel compound over time, leading to significant shifts in behavior and outcomes. As alignment grows, you will notice that decisions feel clearer, opportunities seem to appear more frequently, and you experience greater ease in trusting the path you are on. This is the foundation that supports every practical technique in the chapters ahead, ensuring they work not as isolated tools but as part of a coherent system shaped by both your mind and your emotions.

Raising Your Baseline Vibration in Daily Life

Improving your vibration is often presented as a single moment of transformation, as if one breakthrough meditation or a sudden burst of positivity can permanently shift your state. In reality, what creates lasting change is less dramatic and more consistent: raising your baseline vibration. This is the emotional and energetic level you return to most of the time, even after stress or setbacks. When your baseline rises, you naturally think, feel, and act from a higher place without constant effort. Manifestation becomes easier because alignment is your default rather than something you have to force.

The first step to raising your baseline is understanding what influences it. Emotional states are not random; they are shaped by a combination of physiology, habits, and environment. What you eat, how you sleep, the quality of your relationships, the narratives you tell yourself, and the spaces you spend time in all send subtle signals to your nervous system. Over time, these signals accumulate into patterns that either uplift or drain you. By becoming conscious of these influences, you gain leverage to make small adjustments that lead to big shifts over time.

The Role of Awareness and Small Wins

Awareness allows you to spot patterns that were previously invisible. Many people underestimate how frequently they engage in thoughts or behaviors that keep their vibration low — constant worry, self-criticism, or exposure to environments filled with negativity. Recognizing these patterns is not about judgment but about choice. Once you see them, you can interrupt them and replace them with habits that build stability and resilience.

Small, consistent improvements are far more effective than chasing temporary highs. A single inspiring seminar might feel transformative in the moment, but unless your daily habits reinforce that elevated state, you quickly return to your old baseline. In contrast, adding small, intentional shifts — brief gratitude reflections, regular movement, mindful breathing — gradually reconditions the nervous system to expect well-being rather than stress. This incremental approach is backed by behavioral research showing that sustainable change comes from repetition, not intensity.

Physiological Foundations of Higher Vibration

Your body's state sets the stage for your emotional state. Chronic stress, nutrient deficiencies, or lack of sleep all lower vibration by overactivating the body's survival mechanisms. When you are constantly in fight-or-flight mode, your brain becomes hyper-focused on potential threats, making it nearly impossible to perceive opportunities or maintain optimism. Addressing basic physical needs is not separate from spiritual work; it is the foundation for it. Balanced nutrition, adequate hydration, restorative sleep, and movement that energizes rather than depletes create the physiological conditions for emotional stability.

This mind-body connection is well documented. Research on heart rate variability, a measure of nervous system balance, shows that positive emotions like appreciation and compassion increase coherence between the heart and brain, supporting clearer thinking and improved resilience. Practices that cultivate these emotions — gratitude journaling, loving-kindness meditation, deep breathing — directly influence your physical state, which in turn influences your vibration.

Creating Environments That Support Elevation

Your surroundings either reinforce or undermine your baseline. Environments filled with constant noise, clutter, or negativity train your nervous system to remain on alert. By contrast, spaces that feel calm, organized, and aligned with your goals signal safety and possibility. Even small adjustments, like clearing visual clutter from your workspace or incorporating natural light, can have measurable effects on mood and focus. Practical implementation begins with identifying your personal "anchors" — simple practices that reliably shift your emotional state upward. These anchors vary from person to person. For some, it might be stepping outside for a few minutes of fresh air, listening to music that evokes joy, or writing down three things they appreciate before starting the day. The key is consistency rather than intensity. Repeating small actions that reliably elevate your state conditions the nervous system to return there more quickly, even during stress.

Equally important is learning to recover from dips in vibration without spiraling. Life will continue to present challenges, and expecting constant high energy creates pressure that often backfires. Instead of judging yourself for low moments, practice rapid resets. These can be as simple as pausing to breathe deeply, reframing the meaning of a situation, or shifting focus toward something constructive you can influence. Over time, these micro-resets train your system to stabilize rather than collapse under pressure.

Integrating movement into your routine is another overlooked yet powerful method for raising vibration. Physical activity is not only beneficial for health but also influences mood-regulating neurotransmitters like dopamine and serotonin. The key is choosing movement that feels enjoyable rather than punishing. Walking, stretching, dancing, or mindful forms of exercise like yoga encourage flow states where mind and body reconnect, often leading to fresh insights and renewed energy.

Nutrition and hydration also play subtler but crucial roles. Blood sugar fluctuations, dehydration, and nutrient deficiencies can mimic anxiety or irritability, making it harder to sustain elevated states. Supporting your body with balanced meals and adequate water intake provides the stability needed for emotional alignment. This is not about perfection or rigid diets but about creating a physical foundation that supports rather than undermines your manifestation work.

Relationships form another layer of influence on baseline vibration. The people you interact with most either nurture or deplete your energy. This does not mean avoiding everyone who struggles but becoming intentional about boundaries and support systems. Prioritizing connections where mutual respect and encouragement are present helps reinforce the emotional patterns you are building. Similarly, limiting exposure to environments steeped in negativity — whether in-person or online — creates space for your own energy to rise without constant interference.

Maintaining a higher baseline also requires periodic recalibration. As you grow, what once lifted you might no longer feel expansive, and new practices may resonate more deeply. Checking in regularly with how you feel allows you to adjust rather than fall into autopilot. This evolving approach keeps your practices fresh and aligned with your current goals and emotional state.

Ultimately, raising your baseline is less about achieving a perfect emotional frequency and more about cultivating resilience. When challenges arise, you recover faster. When opportunities appear, you recognize and act on them without hesitation. This steadier internal state is what allows manifestation to move from fleeting moments of alignment to a lasting way of being, where your daily choices, environment, and emotions consistently support the reality you are creating.

Chapter 3: Reprogramming the Subconscious

Where Limiting Beliefs Come From and Why They Persist

Every person carries a set of core beliefs about themselves and the world. These beliefs shape how we interpret events, what opportunities we notice, and how much we allow ourselves to receive. While some beliefs empower us, others quietly limit what we think is possible. These limiting beliefs often operate beneath conscious awareness, making them harder to identify yet highly influential in daily life and in manifestation efforts. Understanding where these beliefs originate and why they persist is essential for transforming them.

Origins in Early Experiences

Most limiting beliefs are formed in childhood, when the brain is especially impressionable. In those formative years, we absorb messages about who we are and how the world works from parents, teachers, peers, and cultural influences. A single comment from an authority figure — "You're not good with money" or "Dreams like that are unrealistic" — can plant a seed that grows into a lifelong pattern of self-doubt. Because children lack the ability to critically evaluate these statements, they often accept them as absolute truth.
Traumatic or highly emotional experiences also shape beliefs. A child who experiences rejection may internalize the idea that they are unworthy of love. Someone who grew up in financial hardship might unconsciously associate wealth with struggle or danger. Over time, these associations become part of the subconscious framework through which all future experiences are filtered.

Reinforcement Through Repetition

Once a belief is formed, the mind tends to seek evidence that confirms it. Psychologists call this confirmation bias. If you believe "I am bad with money," you are more likely to notice moments where you overspend or struggle financially, while overlooking signs of progress. Each piece of confirming evidence strengthens the belief, creating a self-reinforcing loop. This cycle can persist for decades because the mind is more focused on proving itself right than seeking new possibilities.

The environment further reinforces these patterns. If you are surrounded by people who share similar limiting beliefs — coworkers who constantly complain about work, friends who insist success is only for the lucky — their perspectives echo your own, making it harder to imagine alternatives. Cultural narratives also play a role. Messages about scarcity, competition, or fixed identity are common in media and education, subtly shaping expectations about what is realistic or attainable.

Why Limiting Beliefs Feel "True"

Limiting beliefs persist because they feel safe. Even when they create discomfort, they provide predictability. The brain is wired to prefer familiar patterns, even negative ones, because predictability reduces perceived risk. Challenging a limiting belief can feel threatening to the subconscious, as it disrupts the internal model of how the world works. This is why people often sabotage opportunities that contradict their beliefs — a promotion, a healthy relationship, or unexpected abundance — because those experiences do not align with their internal narrative.

Neuroscience offers insight into this phenomenon. The brain's default mode network, active during self-referential thinking, is strongly tied to our identity and personal story. When new information conflicts with this narrative, the brain resists it, interpreting the unfamiliar as unsafe. Without intentional effort to update these patterns, the old narrative continues to run automatically, guiding thoughts, emotions, and behaviors without conscious input.

Identifying limiting beliefs requires slowing down and paying attention to the subtle thoughts and reactions that arise in daily life. These beliefs often reveal themselves in moments of hesitation or discomfort. When you imagine pursuing a goal and feel immediate doubt, the belief beneath the doubt is worth examining. It might sound like an inner voice saying, "I'm not ready," "I don't deserve this," or "People like me don't get opportunities like that." These internal statements often repeat so quietly and frequently that they are mistaken for facts rather than beliefs.

Journaling can be a powerful tool for uncovering these patterns. Writing freely about your goals and paying attention to the fears or objections that surface on the page helps bring unconscious narratives into the open. For example, if you write about wanting financial freedom and notice recurring thoughts about risk or failure, it signals that deeper associations around money may need attention. Once these thoughts are visible, they can be questioned and reframed rather than accepted at face value.

Beliefs are also revealed in the language you use. Phrases like "I always mess things up," "I can never get ahead," or "That's just how I am" point to identity-level programming rather than temporary experiences. Recognizing these statements allows you to distinguish between objective reality and inherited stories. This distinction is crucial because it gives you the power to rewrite the story rather than continue living inside it unconsciously.

Awareness is the first step toward dismantling limiting beliefs, but awareness alone is not enough. These beliefs persist because they are embedded not only in thought but also in emotion and memory. When a belief formed in response to pain or fear, it is often charged with unresolved emotion. Addressing this emotional layer is necessary for lasting change. Practices like visualization, inner dialogue, or guided reflection can help revisit the original moment the belief was created, bringing compassion and new understanding to it. This does not erase the past but transforms the meaning carried forward from it.

Research in cognitive behavioral therapy supports this process of reframing. Studies show that when people actively challenge distorted thoughts and replace them with more balanced perspectives, neural pathways begin to shift. Over time, the brain stops defaulting to the old narrative and adopts the new one as its baseline. This is the same principle that allows empowering beliefs to become second nature once they are reinforced consistently.

It is also important to understand that dismantling limiting beliefs is not about rejecting every doubt or discomfort. Some caution is useful and protective. The work is to differentiate between fear that signals growth and fear that stems from outdated conditioning. When you learn to recognize this difference, you gain freedom to choose rather than react automatically. As you progress through the practices in this book, you will revisit your beliefs repeatedly. Each layer of awareness reveals another opportunity for alignment. Over time, the beliefs that once felt unshakable begin to soften, replaced by perspectives that support rather than hinder your growth. This shift is foundational for manifestation, because when your core story changes, the way you interact with reality changes with it.

Tools to Identify and Dismantle Hidden Mental Blocks

Even when you have a clear vision of what you want, hidden mental blocks can quietly interfere with progress. These blocks are subconscious patterns that act like invisible walls, preventing you from fully believing, receiving, or acting on opportunities. Because they operate beneath awareness, traditional goal-setting or positive thinking rarely addresses them. The good news is that there are practical tools to bring these patterns to the surface and rewire them in ways that support your growth.

Recognizing Hidden Blocks Through Emotional Triggers

One of the simplest ways to locate mental blocks is by paying attention to emotional triggers. When you think about a goal and feel resistance — fear, anger, or a sense of impossibility — that discomfort often points directly to a limiting belief. For instance, if imagining financial success immediately stirs anxiety about judgment from others, there is likely an underlying association between wealth and rejection. Rather than avoiding these feelings, leaning into them with curiosity helps uncover the deeper narrative that needs rewriting.

Keeping a journal of these triggers can reveal recurring themes. Over time, patterns emerge: fear of failure, discomfort with visibility, or a belief that you must struggle to earn anything worthwhile. Once identified, these patterns can be addressed instead of unconsciously shaping your choices.

Using Thought Audits to Reveal Inner Narratives

A thought audit involves observing the automatic thoughts that arise throughout the day, particularly in response to challenges or opportunities. The goal is not to control every thought but to identify repetitive ones that carry a negative charge. A useful method is to pause whenever you feel an emotional shift and write down the thought behind it. Later, review these entries for themes such as "I'm not ready," "I'll mess this up," or "This is too good to be true."

This process mirrors techniques used in cognitive behavioral therapy, where identifying distorted thoughts is the first step toward changing them. By externalizing these thoughts on paper, they lose some of their power and can be examined more objectively. You begin to see them as patterns rather than truths, which opens the door to change.

The Role of Visualization in Block Discovery

Visualization is often associated with creating positive futures, but it can also reveal hidden resistance. When you imagine living your desired reality, pay attention to what feels uncomfortable or unrealistic. If picturing success triggers anxiety rather than excitement, that response signals an unresolved belief that needs attention. Exploring the source of the discomfort — where it originated, what it is protecting you from — often uncovers blocks you were unaware of.

This method works because the subconscious responds vividly to imagery. By immersing yourself in a mental rehearsal of your goal, you bypass rational defenses and allow deeper emotions and beliefs to surface. These insights can then be processed and reframed, turning obstacles into opportunities for healing and growth.

Once a mental block has been identified, the next step is dismantling it in a way that feels sustainable rather than forced. The goal is not to erase the belief by sheer willpower but to replace it with a more supportive narrative that the subconscious can gradually accept. This process works best when approached with patience and repetition, as beliefs that took years to form will not dissolve overnight.

One effective technique is reframing. After identifying a limiting thought, ask whether it is an absolute fact or an interpretation based on past experiences. Often, you will realize that the belief was formed under specific circumstances that no longer apply. For example, if you grew up hearing that "money is always scarce," that statement reflected the reality of your environment at the time, not an unchangeable truth about the world. Reframing allows you to honor where the belief came from while consciously choosing a new perspective, such as "money is a resource I can learn to manage and attract."

Pairing this cognitive shift with emotion strengthens the change. Simply telling yourself a new belief without feeling it rarely creates lasting results. This is where practices like guided visualization or somatic work become valuable. By imagining yourself living the new belief and generating emotions of safety, relief, or excitement, you imprint the new narrative on both mind and body. Research in neuroplasticity supports this approach, showing that repeated emotional experiences physically reshape neural pathways, making the new belief easier to access over time.

Another method involves identifying and challenging protective behaviors linked to the belief. Many limiting patterns are rooted in self-protection; they were created to shield you from pain or disappointment. A belief like "I shouldn't take risks" may have formed after a past failure, serving as a way to avoid repeating the experience. Understanding this protective role allows you to work with compassion rather than resistance. Instead of fighting the belief, you can thank it for trying to keep you safe and guide yourself toward healthier strategies for protection that do not limit growth. Consistency is key in dismantling hidden blocks. Repetition is what tells the subconscious that the new belief is safe and reliable. This is why integrating supportive affirmations, journaling, or short visualization exercises into daily routines is so effective. Even a few minutes of focused alignment each day compounds into significant change over time. The belief does not have to vanish completely for progress to occur; often, simply weakening its grip is enough to open space for new opportunities to emerge.

As blocks begin to dissolve, it is common to encounter moments of discomfort or resistance. This is a sign of growth rather than failure. The subconscious resists unfamiliar patterns because they challenge established identity. Meeting this discomfort with patience and reaffirming your new narrative prevents backsliding into old habits. Over time, what once felt foreign becomes familiar, and what once felt impossible begins to feel natural.

The real transformation happens when supportive beliefs stop feeling like tools you are practicing and start feeling like truths you live by. At this point, manifestation no longer feels like forcing change but like stepping into alignment with who you were capable of being all along.

Installing New Beliefs That Stick (Proven Methods)

Dismantling limiting beliefs creates space for growth, but true transformation comes from what fills that space. Installing empowering beliefs is about building new mental and emotional patterns that feel natural enough to persist under real-life stress. Many people attempt this through simple affirmations or surface-level positivity, only to find themselves reverting to old habits. The reason is that belief change requires more than repetition; it requires alignment between thought, emotion, and action.

A belief is not just an idea you think; it is a conclusion your subconscious has accepted as true based on accumulated evidence and emotional experiences. To create a new belief, you must give your subconscious compelling reasons to adopt it, both intellectually and emotionally. This means pairing rational proof with felt experiences so the belief becomes embodied rather than merely conceptual.

The Role of Emotional Intensity in Belief Formation

Research on memory formation shows that emotionally charged experiences are more likely to be encoded deeply in the brain. This is why a single intense moment — whether painful or joyful — can influence your behavior for years, while hundreds of neutral experiences are forgotten. Applying this principle to belief installation, pairing new thoughts with strong positive emotion accelerates their adoption. Visualizing a goal while genuinely feeling excitement, gratitude, or relief imprints the new belief far more effectively than repeating it without emotion.

Dr. Joe Dispenza's work on neuroplasticity highlights this connection. His studies show that when people combine intention with elevated emotion, they create measurable changes in brain activity and neural connections. In other words, your brain learns faster and more deeply when what you think is reinforced by what you feel. This is why techniques like vivid visualization, gratitude practices, and affirmations work best when they evoke genuine emotion rather than rote repetition.

Bridging the Gap Between Old and New

For many, the biggest obstacle to installing new beliefs is the gap between where they are and where they want to be. If a belief feels too far from current reality — for example, saying "I am wealthy" while struggling with debt — the subconscious rejects it as false. Bridging thoughts can help close this gap. Instead of leaping straight to the end state, create incremental statements like "I am learning to manage money with confidence" or "I am open to receiving opportunities for abundance." These statements feel believable, which reduces resistance and allows gradual upward shifts.

Consistency is key. Neural pathways strengthen through repetition, but repetition must be intentional and varied to avoid fatigue. Combining multiple modalities — written affirmations, spoken statements, visualization, and somatic practices — engages different parts of the brain and reinforces the belief through multiple sensory channels. This layered approach accelerates integration and makes the belief more resilient under stress.

Anchoring Beliefs Through Action

Thought and emotion create the blueprint, but action cements it. When you behave as though the new belief is true, you provide tangible proof to your subconscious. Each aligned action — making a confident decision, setting a boundary, following through on a commitment — becomes evidence that the belief is real. Over time, these actions compound, transforming the belief from a conscious practice into an automatic truth.

Daily integration is where a belief shifts from an abstract concept into a lived experience. The subconscious learns through repetition and familiarity, so weaving the new belief into ordinary moments is crucial. Begin by pairing the belief with existing routines so it becomes part of your daily rhythm. Speaking affirmations while brushing your teeth, visualizing desired outcomes during your commute, or journaling before bed ensures consistent reinforcement without requiring extra time or energy.

Layering sensory input deepens this process. The subconscious responds strongly to multisensory cues, so combine sight, sound, and touch where possible. Writing the belief by hand engages fine motor memory, speaking it aloud activates auditory processing, and pairing it with physical movement, like walking or deep breathing, grounds it in the body. These subtle variations prevent the practice from becoming mechanical and help the belief feel more embodied.

Equally important is celebrating micro-evidence. Each time life reflects back even a small confirmation of the new belief, acknowledge it. If your new belief is "I attract supportive relationships" and someone unexpectedly offers kindness, pause to notice and appreciate it. This act of recognition tells the subconscious, "This is happening," which accelerates integration. Psychologist Teresa Amabile's research on the progress principle demonstrates that recognizing small wins fuels motivation and builds resilience, a principle directly applicable to belief work.

Addressing setbacks is another critical component. Old beliefs may resurface during stress because they are familiar neural pathways. Instead of interpreting this as failure, treat it as part of the rewiring process. When you notice the old narrative returning, consciously interrupt it and reaffirm the new one. Over time, this consistent redirection weakens the old pattern and strengthens the new default.

Community and environment also play powerful roles in reinforcing beliefs. Surrounding yourself with people who embody or support the new belief creates a feedback loop of validation and modeling. Similarly, curating your environment to reflect the belief — whether through reminders, symbols, or the spaces you spend time in — keeps the subconscious aligned. Environmental cues work quietly in the background, influencing behavior without conscious effort.

Finally, patience is essential. Belief change is cumulative rather than instantaneous. The subconscious resists rapid shifts because it prioritizes safety and predictability. Trusting the process and focusing on consistent practice rather than immediate results creates the conditions for deep, lasting transformation. Over time, the belief moves from something you are practicing to something that feels inherently true, shaping not just how you think but how you respond to life.

When this shift occurs, manifestation accelerates naturally. Actions align with intention, emotions reinforce vision, and external reality begins reflecting the internal changes. At that point, you are no longer forcing yourself to "believe"; you are living from a place where the belief is self-evident. This is where lasting change happens — not through a single breakthrough, but through the quiet accumulation of daily choices and repeated alignment over time.

Part II. Core Techniques

With the foundations in place, you are ready to move into the practical methods that bring manifestation to life. This is where clarity, emotional alignment, and belief work begin to translate into tangible practices you can use every day. While the previous chapters prepared the ground, these techniques are the seeds you will plant and nurture to create visible change in your reality.

Core techniques are often misunderstood as quick fixes or magical rituals. Visualization, scripting, and emotional alignment have been reduced in popular culture to oversimplified exercises: closing your eyes and imagining wealth, writing a wish list in a journal, or trying to feel good no matter what. Used this way, they rarely create lasting results. The purpose of this part of the book is to go deeper — to show you how these tools actually work on the brain and body, and how to apply them in ways that are both effective and sustainable.

You will see that these techniques are not separate from the foundational work you have already done; they are extensions of it. Visualization becomes far more powerful when your desires are clearly defined. Scripting gains potency when it reflects beliefs you have consciously chosen to install. Emotional alignment becomes natural when your baseline vibration is elevated. Each method builds on the previous steps, creating a feedback loop where thought, emotion, and action reinforce each other.

This section will also address common challenges that arise when people attempt these practices — doubts that surface during visualization, discomfort when writing scripts that feel "too big," or difficulty maintaining elevated states in the midst of real-life stress. Rather than dismissing these challenges, we will explore them, because they often hold the key to deeper transformation. Understanding why resistance appears allows you to work through it rather than abandon the practice.

By the end of these chapters, you will have a toolkit of methods that feel practical, flexible, and deeply personal. These are not techniques to do once and forget; they are habits to integrate into the rhythm of your life. With consistent practice, they shift not only what you manifest but how you experience yourself in the process.

Chapter 4: Visualization that Actually Works

The Neuroscience of Visualization (How It Rewires the Brain)

Visualization is often described as "seeing" your desired future in your mind's eye, but its power goes far beyond daydreaming. When practiced correctly, visualization activates the brain in ways strikingly similar to real-life experiences, priming your nervous system to recognize and create the conditions for those experiences to occur. Understanding the neuroscience behind this process not only removes the mystery but also shows why visualization can accelerate manifestation when grounded in clear intention and consistent practice.

How the Brain Processes Imagery

The brain does not fully distinguish between imagined and real events. When you visualize an activity vividly — walking into your dream home, speaking confidently in a meeting, holding a published book in your hands — many of the same neural circuits fire as if you were physically experiencing it. This phenomenon has been demonstrated repeatedly in studies on mental rehearsal.

One notable example comes from research conducted by Dr. Guang Yue at the Cleveland Clinic. In this study, participants who mentally rehearsed finger-strength exercises increased their muscle strength by nearly 13 percent, despite never performing the movement physically. Functional MRI scans revealed that the same motor areas of the brain were activated during mental practice as during actual movement. This finding illustrates how visualization can condition the body and mind to perform in alignment with the imagined outcome.

Neuroplasticity and Rewiring Beliefs

At the core of visualization's effectiveness is neuroplasticity — the brain's ability to reorganize itself by forming new neural connections. Every time you vividly imagine your desired future, especially when paired with emotion, you strengthen the neural pathways associated with that reality. Over time, this repetition begins to replace older patterns tied to fear, scarcity, or self-doubt with ones that support confidence and possibility.

This process mirrors how skills are learned in other areas of life. A pianist repeatedly practicing scales physically wires the brain to play them effortlessly. Similarly, visualizing success conditions your brain to view the new outcome as familiar and attainable, reducing resistance when opportunities to act on it appear.

The Role of Emotion in Visualization

While imagery activates the brain, emotion locks it in. Neuroscientist Dr. Antonio Damasio's research on decision-making shows that emotional input is essential for learning and memory formation. When you imagine a goal and pair it with elevated emotions — gratitude, joy, excitement — the brain encodes the experience more deeply. This emotional charge signals to the subconscious that the vision is significant, prompting it to filter daily life for cues that align with the imagined reality.

Without emotion, visualization risks becoming hollow. Many people go through the motions of imagining their goals but remain detached, which limits its impact. The key is to immerse yourself fully, allowing the experience to feel real enough to influence your physiology. Heart rate, breathing patterns, and hormonal responses often shift during vivid visualization, proving that the body responds to imagined events as though they were tangible.

To fully activate the brain's response, visualization must engage multiple senses. Rather than simply picturing a desired outcome, incorporate sound, touch, and even smell to create a richer internal experience. If you are visualizing a new home, imagine the echo of footsteps on the floor, the feel of the door handle, the scent of fresh paint or morning coffee in the kitchen. These sensory details strengthen neural encoding, making the imagined reality feel more familiar and achievable. The more vividly you experience it, the more your subconscious accepts it as a potential reality rather than a distant fantasy.

The timing of visualization also influences its effectiveness. Practicing during relaxed but alert states — such as just after waking or before sleep — leverages the brain's natural receptivity. In these moments, brainwave activity slows, allowing suggestions to bypass critical filters and reach the subconscious more easily. Athletes have long used this window to mentally rehearse performance, and the same principle applies to personal manifestation work. By anchoring visualization to these natural rhythms, you enhance retention and reduce mental resistance.

Repetition is crucial, yet it must remain intentional. Mechanical repetition without emotional engagement can dull the practice, while infrequent visualization fails to create the necessary neural reinforcement. A balanced approach is to commit to short, consistent sessions that feel immersive rather than forced. Even five to ten minutes daily can create significant changes when practiced with focus and feeling. Over time, the brain begins to expect the envisioned reality, priming you to notice opportunities and act in alignment with them.

It is equally important to recognize and address any resistance that arises during visualization. Sometimes imagining a goal triggers discomfort or disbelief, revealing conflicting subconscious beliefs. Instead of ignoring these reactions, acknowledge them as valuable feedback. They highlight areas that may require additional belief work or incremental steps to bridge the gap between current reality and desired outcome. Integrating this insight ensures your visualization practice aligns with deeper emotional truth rather than bypassing it.

Scientific research also supports the cumulative benefits of pairing visualization with real-world action. Studies on mental rehearsal in sports and skill acquisition show that combining visualization with physical practice yields superior results compared to either approach alone. When applied to manifestation, this means that mentally rehearsing a confident presentation, for example, prepares the brain, but actually speaking up in smaller real-life situations reinforces the new neural pathways even more. The synergy between imagined and lived experience accelerates belief change and behavioral alignment.

Ultimately, visualization works because it conditions your nervous system to recognize and embody the future you are creating. It transforms goals from abstract ideas into rehearsed experiences, reducing uncertainty and building confidence. When combined with the emotional and belief work from previous chapters, visualization becomes a bridge between intention and action, preparing both mind and body to step into new realities with less resistance. Practiced consistently, it stops being a separate exercise and becomes a natural part of how you process possibilities, shaping not only what you attract but also how you respond to life itself.

Creating Sensory-Rich Visualizations for Faster Results

Visualization is most powerful when it feels real. The closer your mind can come to simulating the full sensory experience of your desired future, the more effectively it imprints on your subconscious. Many people imagine only in vague pictures — a quick mental snapshot of a new car, a house, or a promotion — but this kind of surface imagery lacks the depth needed to trigger significant change. The key is to activate as many senses as possible so the visualization becomes immersive, convincing your nervous system that the imagined experience is already familiar.

Why Sensory Detail Matters

The brain processes imagined sensory input using similar neural pathways as real experiences. When you vividly hear, feel, and even smell the details of your vision, you strengthen the connections between thought and emotion, which accelerates belief formation. Neuroscience studies on mental rehearsal in athletes confirm this: players who incorporated multiple senses into their visualizations saw greater performance improvements than those who relied solely on visual imagery. The more lifelike the experience, the stronger the imprint.

Sensory-rich visualization also bypasses the mind's tendency to doubt. A simple image of "being wealthy" might trigger disbelief if your current reality feels far from it. But imagining the texture of crisp paper as you count money, the muted hum of a quiet office where you work freely, or the lightness in your chest as bills are easily paid engages the body in ways that logic cannot argue with. The body responds as though the experience is happening now, creating emotional resonance that builds momentum toward the outcome.

Engaging All Senses

Start with the sense most natural to you — often sight — and gradually layer in others. Instead of picturing a vague scene, focus on specifics. What colors dominate the space? How is the lighting? Are you indoors or outside? Then add sound: the subtle background noise of a city street, the murmur of supportive voices, or the quiet rustle of leaves in a place of peace. Next, incorporate touch: the feel of clothing against your skin, the temperature of the air, the texture of objects you interact with. Smell and taste, though less commonly used, can deepen immersion even further. The scent of morning coffee in your dream home or the flavor of a celebratory meal after achieving a goal can anchor the vision in the body's memory.

Bridging Emotion Through Sensation

The purpose of engaging the senses is not just to create a vivid picture but to evoke emotion. Emotions are the fuel that signals to the subconscious, "This is real and important." As you layer sensory detail, notice how your body responds — a sense of warmth in the chest, relaxation in the shoulders, or excitement in the stomach. These reactions are signs that the visualization is influencing not just your thoughts but your physiology, which is where lasting change begins.

Integrating sensory-rich visualization into daily life begins with creating a consistent ritual. The subconscious thrives on repetition, so practicing at the same time each day strengthens the neural pathways associated with your desired reality. Early morning and just before sleep are particularly effective because the brain is naturally in a more suggestible state, allowing images and emotions to bypass resistance and settle deeper. Even five minutes of fully immersive visualization can be more impactful than longer sessions done sporadically.

Depth is more important than duration. Focus on immersing yourself fully rather than rushing to cover every possible detail at once. Choose one scene that represents the essence of your desire — a moment that symbolizes the bigger picture — and enrich it with sensory layers. If you are visualizing career success, you might focus on a single scene of receiving recognition for your work, hearing the applause, feeling the weight of an award in your hands, noticing the fabric of your clothing, and sensing the quiet pride that fills you in that moment. The richness of one scene often resonates more deeply than a vague attempt to picture an entire future.

As you repeat this practice, the emotional response it generates becomes as valuable as the imagery itself. The purpose is not only to create a picture but to anchor your body in the emotional state of already having what you desire. This emotional imprint becomes a guide for your daily actions and decisions. When you know what it feels like to experience freedom, love, or abundance, you are more likely to recognize and pursue opportunities that align with that feeling.

For many people, resistance arises in the form of distraction or disbelief during visualization. Rather than fighting these interruptions, acknowledge them and return gently to the sensory experience. Over time, your ability to stay present will improve. If disbelief feels particularly strong, adjust the visualization to a scenario that feels slightly more attainable — an incremental step toward your ultimate vision — until your nervous system acclimates to the new emotional state.

Pairing visualization with other practices can amplify its effects. Writing a brief script of what you are visualizing before or after the session helps reinforce the imagery in a different modality. Gratitude journaling can be combined with visualization by reflecting on the emotions you felt during the practice and expressing thanks for them as if they are already part of your reality. These layered approaches engage multiple parts of the brain, creating a stronger imprint.

The ultimate goal is for these sensory-rich visualizations to become second nature. When you can evoke the sights, sounds, and feelings of your future on command, you begin to experience that future as familiar rather than distant. This familiarity reduces hesitation when real-life opportunities arise because the subconscious already accepts the experience as part of your identity. Over time, this alignment between imagined and actual experiences accelerates both inner and outer transformation, bridging the gap between intention and manifestation in a way that feels natural and sustainable.

Common Visualization Mistakes and How to Fix Them

Visualization is one of the most powerful tools for manifestation, yet many people practice it in ways that limit its impact. The technique itself is simple, but subtle errors can prevent the brain and body from fully engaging with the experience. These mistakes are common because most advice on visualization remains superficial, focusing on quick tips rather than the underlying mechanics of how the mind integrates imagined experiences. By understanding where people go wrong, you can avoid wasted effort and ensure every session moves you closer to your desired reality.

Mistake 1: Treating Visualization as Daydreaming

One of the biggest misconceptions is thinking that visualization is the same as casually imagining something pleasant. Daydreaming drifts without focus, while effective visualization is deliberate and immersive. The brain must believe the imagined scene is relevant enough to encode it, which only happens when you bring specificity and emotion into the practice. Without those elements, the session might feel nice in the moment but rarely leads to lasting change because it fails to create the neural connections needed for belief.

The fix is to approach visualization as rehearsal rather than fantasy. Instead of passively watching yourself succeed, step into the scene and experience it through your own senses. Feel the textures, hear the sounds, notice the emotional response in your body. This level of involvement signals to the subconscious that the experience matters and should be stored as a reference point for future behavior.

Mistake 2: Visualizing Outcomes Without Emotional Engagement

Many people focus exclusively on the picture of what they want but forget to engage with how it feels. The emotional component is what activates deeper areas of the brain responsible for motivation and memory. Without it, visualization becomes hollow and mechanical. A vivid mental image of holding a book you have authored will not create momentum unless you also feel the pride, relief, or joy that would accompany that moment.

To correct this, shift your focus to the emotions underlying your desire. Ask yourself what feelings you believe the outcome will give you — freedom, security, love, excitement — and emphasize those during visualization. The stronger the emotional resonance, the faster the subconscious adopts the new belief as possible and begins filtering reality in alignment with it.

Mistake 3: Overcomplicating or Forcing the Process

Another common pitfall is turning visualization into a rigid, overly detailed routine. While specificity helps, obsessing over perfect accuracy can trigger stress rather than alignment. People often feel pressure to picture every detail exactly the same way each time, worrying that any variation will "ruin" the manifestation. This approach creates tension and can even amplify self-doubt if the mind resists elements that feel unrealistic.

The solution is to focus on the essence rather than perfection. Choose one or two anchor moments that symbolize your goal — such as crossing a finish line, signing a contract, or embracing a loved one — and allow details to evolve naturally. This flexibility prevents the practice from feeling like a chore and keeps it emotionally authentic.

Another frequent error is visualizing too far ahead of what feels believable. When the desired outcome feels completely disconnected from current reality, the subconscious can reject the experience outright. This often shows up as inner dialogue like "this will never happen" or physical discomfort while visualizing. For example, picturing yourself as a millionaire while struggling to pay bills may create more tension than inspiration, which interrupts the neural imprint you are trying to build.

The way to correct this is by using incremental visualization. Rather than jumping straight to the ultimate goal, begin with scenarios that represent believable milestones. If the end vision is complete financial freedom, visualize first receiving a new client, landing a better-paying job, or seeing your savings account steadily grow. As these intermediate goals begin to feel real, the larger vision becomes easier to embody. Over time, the subconscious bridges the gap and accepts the bigger picture without resistance.

A related mistake is visualizing only the outcome and ignoring the process that leads to it. While imagining the end result creates motivation, it can also set up unrealistic expectations if you do not mentally rehearse the steps needed to reach it. Athletes, for instance, do not only visualize winning; they also picture themselves executing precise movements under pressure. This dual focus strengthens both confidence and preparedness. Applying the same principle to personal goals means visualizing yourself taking aligned actions — making the call, attending the meeting, practicing the skill — as well as enjoying the outcome itself.

Another subtle trap is inconsistency. Many people visualize intensely for a short period, then stop when results do not appear immediately. This on-and-off approach prevents the brain from building strong enough neural connections for lasting change. Visualization works best as part of a daily rhythm, much like physical training. Even short, regular sessions compound over time, gradually shifting both perception and behavior. The fix is to commit to manageable consistency rather than bursts of intensity. A few focused minutes each day are more effective than sporadic hour-long sessions.

One of the less obvious mistakes is neglecting to update the visualization as you grow. Goals evolve, and what once felt inspiring may eventually feel stale. If you keep replaying the same scene long after it no longer resonates, the practice loses its emotional charge. Periodically refreshing the imagery ensures it stays aligned with your current desires and emotional state. This could mean adding new details, adjusting the environment, or choosing a different symbolic moment that better reflects your evolving goals.

Finally, many people forget to integrate visualization into daily life beyond formal practice sessions. The most powerful shifts occur when the emotional state cultivated during visualization carries over into real-time decisions and interactions. By intentionally recalling the feelings of your vision throughout the day — before a meeting, during a challenging moment, or while making choices — you reinforce alignment and begin living as if the desired reality is already unfolding. This continuity between practice and daily action is what transforms visualization from a mental exercise into a lived experience.

Chapter 5: The Art of Scripting

Writing Your Reality as if It Already Exists

Scripting is the practice of writing about your desired future in the present tense, as though it has already happened. Rather than describing what you hope for, you describe what you are living. This technique blends the power of visualization with the clarity of language, transforming vague desires into vivid narratives that your subconscious can recognize and adopt. When done correctly, scripting bridges the gap between thought and embodiment, training the mind and emotions to align with the reality you are creating.

Why Writing in the Present Works

The subconscious mind responds more strongly to immediacy than to future projections. Writing "I will be successful" signals to the mind that success is always ahead, never now. Writing "I am successful" tells the subconscious that this is your current identity, prompting it to organize thoughts, behaviors, and perceptions accordingly. This is supported by research on self-affirmation theory, which shows that present-tense affirmations create measurable changes in behavior when they reflect values a person genuinely holds or is moving toward.

There is also a neurological advantage to writing rather than only thinking or speaking. The act of physically writing engages multiple regions of the brain, including those responsible for motor control, memory, and emotional processing. This multisensory involvement strengthens the imprint of the desired belief and reinforces neural pathways more effectively than mental rehearsal alone.

Creating a Compelling Narrative

The most effective scripts go beyond listing goals; they tell a story. A simple statement like "I am abundant" may feel hollow or forced if it lacks context. A narrative, on the other hand, paints a scene: waking up in a peaceful home, feeling gratitude for supportive relationships, experiencing the freedom of financial stability. This storytelling approach mirrors the way the brain naturally encodes memories, making the imagined experience more convincing and easier to recall.

When crafting your script, focus on emotional resonance rather than perfection. Write in a way that makes you feel something as you read it back. The goal is not to create a flawless piece of prose but to immerse yourself in the feelings of living the reality you want. Emotions are what tell the subconscious, "This is important." Without them, the words remain surface-level.

Combining Scripting with Sensory Detail

To deepen impact, include sensory cues in your writing. Instead of saying, "I drive my dream car," describe the weight of the steering wheel, the smell of new leather, the quiet hum of the engine. These details engage the same neural pathways as visualization, transforming abstract goals into felt experiences. The richer the sensory description, the more familiar the desired reality becomes to your nervous system, and the easier it is to take aligned action in real life.

Building scripting into daily life works best when it becomes a ritual rather than an occasional exercise. Set aside a few minutes each morning or evening to connect with your vision and put it into words. The regularity matters more than the length; even a single page written consistently carries more weight than sporadic sessions that try to do too much at once. Over time, the practice turns into a mental habit — your default narrative begins to shift toward possibility and alignment rather than doubt or scarcity.

The tone of your scripting is equally important. Write with a sense of calm confidence rather than desperation or forced optimism. Instead of trying to convince yourself of something you do not believe, allow the narrative to reflect the version of you who naturally lives the reality you are describing. This might mean softening language when needed — writing "I feel supported and open to opportunities for wealth" can be more powerful than rigidly declaring "I am a millionaire" if the latter feels untrue and triggers resistance. Incremental upgrades in language often create more lasting belief than giant leaps that the subconscious cannot accept.

Another effective method is revisiting and refining your scripts over time. As you grow and evolve, your goals and emotional states may shift. Updating your writing keeps it relevant and prevents it from becoming stale.

Reading old scripts can also be a powerful motivator, revealing how much progress you have made and how previous visions have already started materializing. This reflection builds trust in the process, reinforcing the connection between what you write and what unfolds in your life.

Pairing scripting with complementary practices amplifies its effects. Reading your script aloud after writing engages auditory processing and strengthens the emotional imprint. Visualizing scenes from your script adds another layer of neural reinforcement, while expressing gratitude for the experiences described helps integrate them emotionally. This multisensory approach transforms scripting from a purely mental activity into a full-bodied practice that engages thought, feeling, and physical awareness.

Addressing doubt when it arises is essential. It is normal for skepticism to surface, especially in the early stages when external circumstances have not yet caught up to the internal vision. Rather than resisting these doubts, acknowledge them and return to the feeling state you are cultivating. Over time, as small manifestations begin to appear, the doubts naturally weaken. Each confirmation — even subtle ones — strengthens your trust that the narrative you are writing is already in motion.

The most profound shift happens when scripting no longer feels like imagining a distant dream but like documenting a reality you are steadily stepping into. At this stage, the practice stops being about forcing belief and becomes about maintaining alignment. You no longer write to escape your current life; you write to deepen your connection to the life you are actively living into. This shift marks the point where manifestation stops feeling abstract and begins unfolding as a natural extension of who you are becoming.

How to Build Emotion and Believability into Your Scripts

The effectiveness of scripting depends not just on what you write but on how believable and emotionally charged it feels. A beautifully written script that feels hollow will not penetrate the subconscious because there is no emotional signal to mark it as important. Similarly, a script that feels forced or unrealistic can trigger resistance rather than alignment. The goal is to create writing that feels inspiring and attainable, evoking genuine feelings that your mind and body can accept as real.

Why Emotion Is Essential

Emotion is the bridge between thought and embodiment. Neuroscientific studies on memory formation show that emotionally charged events are encoded more deeply in the brain than neutral ones. When you write a script and feel gratitude, excitement, or relief as though the event is happening now, the subconscious processes it as a lived experience. This emotional intensity is what begins to shift neural pathways and anchor the new belief as part of your identity.

Without emotion, scripting becomes mechanical. Writing "I am confident and successful" without feeling it will have little impact because the body does not register the statement as meaningful. Bringing emotion into the practice is not about faking happiness; it is about connecting with the genuine feelings you expect the outcome to bring. If the script describes financial security, focus on the calm and freedom you would feel waking up without financial stress, rather than just the number in your bank account.

The Role of Believability

Believability determines whether the subconscious accepts or rejects the script. If the statement feels too far removed from current reality, the mind resists. For example, if someone struggling to pay rent writes "I have ten million dollars," the gap can be so wide that disbelief overshadows the practice. In contrast, writing "I am steadily growing my income and attracting new opportunities" bridges the gap between where they are and where they want to be. This incremental approach builds confidence, allowing the subconscious to gradually accept bigger truths as evidence accumulates.

One strategy for enhancing believability is focusing on experiences rather than numbers or titles. Instead of writing "I am CEO of a major company," write about what it feels like to lead a team you love, make impactful decisions, and feel respected for your vision. By emphasizing the emotional essence rather than rigid specifics, you create space for the subconscious to embrace the feeling of success even if the exact form evolves over time.

Blending Emotion and Believability

The most powerful scripts combine authentic emotion with statements that feel possible, even if they stretch your comfort zone. Begin by identifying the core feeling behind your goal — security, freedom, love, purpose — and weave that into your writing. Pair it with vivid sensory details that make the scene come alive: the quiet of a peaceful morning, the texture of a handwritten book contract, the sound of supportive applause. When the words evoke a physical response, like warmth in the chest or a relaxed breath, you know the script is resonating.

Strengthening emotional resonance starts with repetition, but not in the mechanical sense of copying the same words over and over. Each time you return to the script, allow yourself to reconnect with the feelings it evokes rather than focusing on memorizing exact sentences. The point is to deepen immersion, not to perfect the language. Over time, this emotional familiarity helps dissolve the gap between where you are and the reality you are writing about, making the new belief feel like a natural extension of your identity.

Incorporating gratitude amplifies this effect. Gratitude signals to the brain that something valuable is already present, which shifts the nervous system toward receptivity rather than longing. Ending your script with a note of thankfulness — "I am so grateful to be living this reality" — conditions the body to relax into the vision instead of chasing it. This subtle shift turns scripting from a wishful exercise into a declaration of presence, a quiet certainty that what you are describing is unfolding now.

Another way to enhance believability is layering real-life evidence into your script. As you notice small signs of progress — an unexpected opportunity, a supportive conversation, a slight increase in confidence — integrate them into your writing. This creates a feedback loop: the script reinforces the evidence, and the evidence reinforces the script. Gradually, the narrative you are writing begins to match what you see around you, which further strengthens trust in the process.

Adjusting scripts as you evolve prevents them from feeling stale. As you achieve milestones, update your writing to reflect the next stage of your vision. If your original script described feeling confident in job interviews, later scripts might focus on thriving in your new role or leading projects with ease. This evolving practice mirrors your growth and maintains alignment with your current aspirations rather than anchoring you to past goals.

Believability also improves when you engage the body during scripting. Speaking the words aloud after writing activates a different part of the brain, while reading them with intentional breathing deepens relaxation and emotional connection. Some people find value in pairing scripting with movement, such as walking or stretching, to integrate the practice physically. These subtle actions communicate safety and presence to the nervous system, allowing the new belief to settle more fully.

Consistency is what transforms scripting from a tool into a habit that reshapes identity. Daily engagement is ideal, but even a few times a week can create change when done with focus and feeling. Over time, the emotional responses you cultivate during scripting will start appearing spontaneously during your day — moments where you feel calm, confident, or inspired without needing to try. This is the clearest sign the subconscious has accepted the new narrative.

When your scripts carry both strong emotion and believable narratives, they stop feeling like exercises and start functioning as living blueprints. They not only describe what you want but help you become the person capable of living it. This alignment between thought, feeling, and behavior is where manifestation begins moving from effortful practice to natural expression.

Daily and Weekly Scripting Routines for Results

Scripting becomes transformative when it shifts from a one-time exercise into a consistent rhythm woven into your life. Sporadic writing can create momentary inspiration, but it rarely produces lasting results. The subconscious changes through repeated exposure to new patterns, and daily and weekly routines ensure that the vision you are cultivating stays alive in your awareness. The goal is not to add another rigid task to your schedule but to create simple, sustainable practices that align naturally with your days.

The Role of Daily Scripting

Daily scripting is about immersion. Each day offers an opportunity to reconnect with your vision and remind your mind and body of where you are heading. These sessions do not have to be long; even five to ten minutes can be enough to anchor your focus and shift your emotional state. What matters most is the quality of your engagement — feeling what you write, believing in it as you put it into words, and carrying that emotional tone into the rest of your day.

One effective approach is to write in the morning. Early hours provide a clean mental slate before the demands of the day set in, making it easier to align with your vision without competing distractions. Writing in the morning also influences how you interpret events throughout the day. When your first thoughts are centered on abundance, connection, or purpose, you are more likely to notice opportunities and respond to challenges with clarity rather than reactivity.

Evening scripting serves a different purpose. Writing before bed helps release the weight of the day and shifts your focus to what you are creating rather than what you lack. Because the subconscious processes information during sleep, ending your day with a vivid, positive narrative allows those images and feelings to settle deeper. Many people find value in combining morning and evening scripting — a brief session to set the tone and another to reinforce it — but even choosing one time consistently can produce meaningful results.

Weekly Deep-Dive Sessions

While daily scripting keeps you connected, weekly sessions allow for broader reflection and refinement. These longer sessions are an opportunity to review your progress, acknowledge any shifts you have noticed, and update your vision as it evolves. You can revisit your earlier writings, identify recurring themes, and expand on details that now feel clearer. This weekly check-in also provides space to celebrate small wins, which strengthens belief and motivation by reinforcing evidence that the process is working.

Weekly sessions are especially helpful for identifying resistance. If doubts or recurring fears appear in your daily writing, use the longer weekly practice to explore them. Rather than pushing resistance aside, acknowledge it and write through it. This might mean reframing a belief, clarifying why a particular goal matters, or breaking a large vision into smaller, more approachable steps. Addressing resistance directly ensures it does not silently undermine your daily efforts.

Structuring these routines works best when there is a balance between consistency and flexibility. Daily sessions should feel light and approachable, something you look forward to rather than dread. A simple structure is to begin with a grounding moment — a few deep breaths to quiet the mind — followed by writing a scene from your desired reality as if it is unfolding now. Choose one or two core themes to focus on each day rather than trying to cover every possible goal. This keeps the writing fresh and prevents overwhelm while still reinforcing your larger vision.

Weekly sessions can expand on this framework by incorporating reflection. Set aside uninterrupted time, ideally on the same day each week, to review your daily scripts and notice patterns. Ask yourself what feels stronger, what feels less believable, and what progress has shown up in subtle ways. Use this insight to refine your vision so it remains aligned with your evolving priorities. This is also an ideal moment to acknowledge small external confirmations — signs that your internal work is beginning to manifest. Recognition of these moments strengthens trust and keeps motivation alive.

One challenge many people face is monotony. Writing similar ideas every day can begin to feel repetitive, which dulls emotional engagement. To counter this, vary your approach. Some days you might write a detailed scene; other days you might write a letter to your future self or a journal entry from the perspective of already living your dream life. Experimenting with tone and format keeps the practice dynamic while maintaining the core principle of writing in the present tense.

It is equally important to manage expectations. Scripting is not about forcing immediate results but about gradually reshaping your internal state so that your external actions and decisions naturally shift. Trust builds as you notice incremental changes: a calmer response to stress, a sudden idea that feels aligned, or opportunities appearing where you previously saw none. These subtle shifts are signs the subconscious is integrating the narrative you are writing.

Integrating these routines into daily life does not require isolating yourself from everything else. In fact, the most profound results occur when scripting influences how you show up in ordinary moments. Carry the emotional tone of your writing into conversations, choices, and habits. When a challenge arises, recall the feeling state you cultivated during scripting and respond from that place rather than from old patterns. Over time, this alignment between what you write and how you live creates a self-reinforcing loop that accelerates manifestation.

Above all, consistency matters more than perfection. Missing a day or feeling less inspired occasionally does not undo the work you have done. What shapes your reality is the overall trend of repeatedly immersing yourself in your chosen vision until it becomes familiar. When that familiarity takes root, scripting stops feeling like an exercise and starts functioning as a natural way of relating to your future — one that continually shapes the decisions you make and the opportunities you perceive.

Chapter 6: Emotional Alignment in Real Life

Handling Doubt, Fear, and Low-Energy States Without Resetting Progress

No matter how committed you are to manifestation practices, moments of doubt and low energy are inevitable. These experiences do not mean you are failing or moving backward; they are part of the natural ebb and flow of growth. The real challenge is not eliminating doubt or fear altogether but learning how to navigate them without letting them derail your progress. When you understand that low-energy states are temporary and manageable, you gain the ability to stay aligned even in difficult moments.

Why Doubt and Fear Arise

Doubt and fear often emerge when your external reality has not yet caught up with your internal vision. You may be writing, visualizing, and aligning daily, yet the physical evidence of change feels slow to appear. The mind naturally questions whether the effort is working, and old beliefs resurface. Fear can also stem from stepping outside familiar comfort zones; even positive change triggers uncertainty because it challenges long-standing patterns. Recognizing these responses as normal reduces their power over you.
Another reason low-energy states appear is simple physiology. Fatigue, poor sleep, and stress deplete emotional resilience, making it harder to maintain high vibration or optimism. This is why manifestation work must include attention to the basics of physical and emotional well-being. A balanced nervous system supports consistent alignment, while an overstressed body can magnify fears that would otherwise feel manageable.

The Myth of "Resetting" Progress

A common misconception is that experiencing fear or negativity cancels out previous manifestation work. People worry that one bad day or one doubtful thought will undo months of alignment. This belief creates unnecessary pressure and often leads to shame, which lowers energy even further. The truth is that progress is cumulative. Each time you return to your practices after a setback, you strengthen resilience and prove to yourself that alignment is not fragile but adaptable.

The brain learns through repetition, not perfection. Neural pathways formed through visualization, scripting, and emotional alignment do not vanish the moment you feel discouraged. They are reinforced each time you return to them. In fact, navigating doubt successfully deepens your belief because it shows you can stay the course even when conditions are less than ideal.

Responding Instead of Reacting

The key to managing doubt and fear is to respond rather than react. Reacting means getting pulled into the story of the emotion — believing every anxious thought and spiraling into worst-case scenarios. Responding involves noticing the feeling, acknowledging it, and choosing a supportive action. This pause creates space between stimulus and response, allowing you to shift your state without suppressing what you feel.

Simple grounding techniques can help create that pause. Slowing your breath, stepping outside for fresh air, or briefly focusing on physical sensations brings you back to the present moment. Once calm is restored, you can use reframing questions like "What else could be true?" or "What evidence do I have that progress is unfolding?" These shifts do not deny the challenge but remind your mind that your current feeling is not the whole story.

Building long-term resilience begins with accepting that alignment is not a fixed state but a skill that strengthens through practice. Each time you navigate a dip in energy or confidence, you train yourself to return to balance more quickly. Over time, the distance between low moments and recovery shortens, and setbacks feel less threatening. This shift is what allows manifestation to become sustainable rather than dependent on fleeting bursts of motivation.

One of the most effective ways to reinforce this resilience is through intentional self-talk. The inner dialogue you use during difficult moments determines whether you deepen doubt or reorient toward trust. Phrases like "This is temporary," "I've handled this before," or "I can shift how I feel" signal safety to the nervous system and remind you that the current moment does not define your future. When repeated consistently, these affirmations evolve from conscious reminders into automatic responses that surface naturally when challenges arise.

Supporting emotional balance also requires attention to the body. Doubt and fear often feel amplified when the nervous system is overstimulated. Incorporating grounding practices — deep breathing, progressive muscle relaxation, or even brief periods of silence — can calm physiological stress and make it easier to return to a centered state. These practices do not eliminate the thought patterns behind fear but create enough stability for you to address them with clarity.

Reframing low-energy periods as opportunities for insight transforms how you relate to them. Instead of viewing fear as a sign of failure, treat it as feedback. Ask what the emotion is pointing to: Is there an old belief that still needs healing? Is there a practical change you have been avoiding? Fear often highlights areas where growth is possible, and addressing it directly turns what once felt like an obstacle into a source of progress.

A helpful practice is journaling specifically about the low-energy state. Writing down what you feel without judgment allows emotions to move rather than stagnate. Once the intensity softens, you can pivot the narrative toward solutions or affirmations that reestablish alignment. This simple process of expression followed by redirection is powerful because it honors the emotion while guiding it toward resolution rather than suppression.

Consistency in your core manifestation practices is equally important during low-energy periods. Even if your visualizations or scripts feel less inspired, continuing them reinforces commitment to your vision. These moments are when habits matter most — not because you need to force enthusiasm but because steady action signals to your subconscious that the vision remains your chosen path regardless of temporary emotions. Progress continues quietly beneath the surface, even if you cannot feel it in the moment.

Ultimately, the measure of growth is not whether doubt disappears but how you handle it when it arises. When you learn to observe fear without becoming consumed by it, to pause rather than spiral, and to return to alignment without judgment, you break the cycle of self-sabotage that derails most people. This is where true stability emerges — the kind that carries you through challenges and keeps you moving steadily toward the reality you are creating.

How to Use Contrast (Bad Days) as a Manifestation Tool

Bad days are often misunderstood in the context of manifestation. Many people believe that negative emotions or challenging experiences undo their progress or block their desires. In reality, contrast — the experience of something unwanted — is not a setback but a critical part of the manifestation process. It reveals where misalignment still exists, clarifies what you truly want, and strengthens your ability to hold vision even when reality does not yet reflect it.

Understanding the Value of Contrast

Contrast is what helps you define your desires with precision. Without it, goals remain vague. When you encounter frustration at work, for example, you gain clarity about the kind of career environment you want instead: supportive colleagues, meaningful projects, greater freedom. When you feel loneliness, you sharpen your understanding of the connection you seek. Contrast acts like a mirror, reflecting both what you do not want and, by extension, what you deeply value.

This shift in perspective is crucial. Instead of interpreting discomfort as failure, you begin to view it as feedback. Every negative emotion signals an unmet need or a misaligned belief. Recognizing this turns difficult moments into data — not proof that manifestation is failing, but guidance on where to focus your energy.

Why Most People Resist Contrast

Many avoid contrast because they fear it will reinforce negativity. They try to push away bad days, ignore difficult feelings, or force positivity. This avoidance often backfires. Suppressed emotions linger beneath the surface and influence behavior in subtle ways. Worse, denying contrast deprives you of the opportunity to gain insight from it.

Facing discomfort directly does not mean wallowing in it. It means observing it without judgment and asking what it is teaching you. This perspective aligns with research on emotional resilience, which shows that acknowledging negative feelings — rather than suppressing them — helps people recover more quickly and respond more constructively to challenges.

Reframing Bad Days as Opportunities

The first step in using contrast as a tool is reframing what it represents. A bad day does not erase progress; it highlights the gap between where you are and where you want to be. That gap is valuable because it points directly to the adjustments needed for alignment. Instead of spiraling into frustration, you can shift into curiosity: What is this moment showing me about my desires? What is it revealing about old patterns I am ready to release?

This approach prevents you from identifying with temporary emotions. Feeling discouraged does not mean you are a discouraged person; it means something in your environment or belief system needs attention. When you separate identity from emotion, you create space to respond intentionally rather than react impulsively.

Turning Awareness into Clarity

Once you recognize the message in contrast, you can use it to refine your vision. Write down what triggered the discomfort, then flip it into a statement of what you want instead. If a tense conversation at work leaves you drained, the desire might be for mutual respect and open communication. If financial stress surfaces, the desire might be for stability and trust in your ability to create it. This process transforms negative experiences into fuel for clearer, more aligned goals.

Integrating contrast into your manifestation practice begins with observation rather than reaction. When discomfort arises, resist the urge to immediately fix or escape it. Instead, pause and acknowledge what you are feeling. This mindful recognition prevents the emotion from escalating and allows you to extract its message. You might silently name the feeling — frustration, fear, disappointment — and then ask what triggered it. This simple process interrupts spirals and converts raw emotion into insight.

Once the message is clear, redirect attention toward its counterpart — the desire that the contrast revealed. Writing this out can be especially powerful. A simple practice is to keep a "contrast journal" where each negative experience is followed by a positive statement of what you want instead. For example, "I feel unsupported at work" becomes "I thrive in an environment where my contributions are valued." Over time, these reframed statements become building blocks for your visualizations and scripts, ensuring your practices are rooted in clarity rather than vague longing.

It is equally important to release the emotional charge of the contrast once you have gathered its lesson. Holding onto frustration while affirming what you want sends mixed signals to the subconscious. Techniques such as deep breathing, gratitude reflection, or a brief visualization of your preferred outcome help reset your state. The goal is not to deny the contrast but to allow it to inform you and then let it pass, leaving you clearer and calmer than before.

Another way to use contrast is as a benchmark for growth. When similar challenges arise in the future, notice how your response evolves. A situation that once triggered anxiety might now evoke curiosity or determination. These shifts are evidence of internal progress, even if external circumstances have not yet fully changed. Recognizing this growth reinforces confidence and helps you trust the process, which is critical when manifestation feels slower than expected.

Contrast also highlights areas where action is required. Sometimes discomfort signals a need for inner alignment, but other times it points to practical steps you can take immediately. If financial stress arises, the aligned response might include both rewriting limiting beliefs and creating a realistic budget. If tension surfaces in relationships, the insight may lead to clearer communication or healthier boundaries. Using contrast as both emotional and practical guidance ensures that your manifestation process remains grounded and results-oriented.

Over time, this approach transforms how you view challenges. Instead of seeing bad days as setbacks, you begin to recognize them as catalysts — moments that refine your vision and strengthen your resilience. The gap between what you want and what you experience no longer feels like failure; it becomes the space where growth happens. This perspective shift alone reduces resistance and allows you to stay aligned even during life's inevitable fluctuations.

When contrast is embraced rather than feared, manifestation ceases to depend on perfect conditions. You learn to create from within, regardless of external circumstances. This inner steadiness allows your desired reality to emerge more quickly, because you are no longer waiting for life to feel perfect before you engage with it fully. You are practicing alignment in real time, even in the middle of the messiness, which is where transformation truly begins.

Emotional Reset Techniques You Can Use Anytime

Emotional alignment is at the heart of manifestation, yet no one can remain in a perfect state of positivity all the time. Life presents stress, unexpected challenges, and moments of overwhelm that pull your energy downward. What matters most is not avoiding these dips but learning how to recover quickly and naturally. Emotional reset techniques are designed to interrupt negative spirals, calm the nervous system, and restore clarity so you can continue aligning with your vision without losing momentum.

Why Quick Resets Work

The nervous system responds to emotions in real time, influencing heart rate, breathing, and even hormone levels. When stress or fear spikes, the body enters a survival state, narrowing focus and making it difficult to see opportunities or feel hope. A quick reset interrupts this pattern by signaling safety to the body, which allows the mind to shift from reaction to intentional choice. Over time, practicing resets trains you to recover faster, making emotional fluctuations less disruptive to your manifestation process.

The Power of Awareness

The first step in any emotional reset is noticing when you need one. Many people operate on autopilot, unaware that their mood has shifted until frustration has already colored their entire day. Cultivating awareness through brief check-ins helps catch emotions early, when they are easier to redirect. A simple practice is pausing for a few seconds several times a day to ask, "Where is my energy right now?" This creates space to intervene before negativity builds momentum.

Grounding Through Breath

One of the most immediate ways to reset is through controlled breathing. Deep, intentional breaths activate the parasympathetic nervous system, which calms the body's stress response. A technique as simple as inhaling slowly for four counts, holding for four, and exhaling for six can shift your physiology within minutes. The longer exhale signals to your body that it is safe, easing tension and quieting anxious thoughts. This practice can be done anywhere — at your desk, in a car, or even in a crowded space — without anyone noticing.

Using Sensory Anchors

Engaging the senses pulls attention out of mental loops and into the present moment. Sensory anchors can include placing your hand on your heart and noticing the warmth, feeling the texture of an object nearby, or focusing on ambient sounds around you. These small shifts remind your body that it is here and now, not trapped in past memories or imagined future worries. Sensory techniques are especially effective during sudden stress, when thoughts are too fast to rationalize.

Movement to Release Stagnation

Emotions often linger because they are stored physically in the body. Gentle movement — stretching, walking, shaking out the arms — helps release this tension and create a sense of flow. Even a minute of standing up, rolling the shoulders, and shifting posture can transform how you feel. When combined with intentional breathing, movement becomes a powerful reset that clears both mental and physical heaviness.

Mental reframing is one of the fastest ways to shift emotional state when a negative thought pattern has taken hold. Instead of fighting the thought, acknowledge it and look for a broader perspective. Asking questions like "What else could this mean?" or "What could this be teaching me?" turns obstacles into information. Reframing is not about forced positivity but about finding a more balanced interpretation that allows you to move forward without being weighed down by the initial reaction.

Gratitude is another powerful reset because it directly shifts focus from what is lacking to what is already working. In moments of frustration, listing even three things you appreciate — however small — signals abundance to the nervous system and creates a sense of safety. Gratitude does not erase challenges but expands your awareness beyond them, which is often enough to ease tension and restore perspective. Neuroscientific research has shown that consistent gratitude practices can rewire the brain toward greater resilience and optimism, which reinforces long-term alignment with manifestation goals.

Visualization can also be repurposed as a reset tool rather than just a future-planning exercise. Instead of picturing a distant dream, imagine a brief scene that evokes calm or confidence. This could be a memory of a peaceful place, the feeling of a supportive hug, or a moment when you overcame a similar challenge in the past. The goal is not to escape reality but to remind your body what safety and alignment feel like so you can return to that state more easily.

Affirmations, when used carefully, can anchor a reset in words. The key is to choose statements that feel true enough to believe in the moment. If saying "I am completely calm" feels unrealistic while in the midst of panic, shift to "I am finding my calm" or "I can take one step toward ease." These softer affirmations bypass resistance and gently guide your mind toward a better state rather than demanding an instant transformation.

Sometimes the quickest reset comes from changing the environment entirely. Stepping outside, seeking natural light, or moving to a quieter space signals to the body that a shift has occurred. Even a small change, like opening a window or adjusting posture, can break the association with the triggering moment and create a sense of possibility. When combined with intentional breath or gratitude, environmental shifts can create a full reset in just a few minutes.

The most important aspect of these techniques is practice. Emotional regulation is a skill, and the more you use these tools, the more automatic they become. Over time, what once required conscious effort turns into an instinctive response. Instead of spiraling into fear or frustration for hours, you notice the shift quickly, apply a technique, and return to alignment in minutes. This is not about never feeling negative emotions; it is about mastering the art of recovery so you can stay connected to your vision regardless of circumstances.

When you build the ability to reset anytime, manifestation becomes more stable. You no longer rely on perfect moods or external validation to feel aligned. You create a foundation of inner steadiness that supports every practice in this book, allowing progress to continue quietly even in the midst of life's inevitable ups and downs.

Part III. Integration

Up to this point, you have built a foundation of clarity, shifted limiting beliefs, and learned core techniques to align thought and emotion with the reality you want to create. These are powerful skills on their own, but the true transformation happens when they are woven into daily life. Integration is where manifestation stops being something you "do" and becomes the lens through which you live.

Many people experience a surge of inspiration when they first learn manifestation techniques but struggle to maintain momentum once the initial excitement fades. They visualize for a few weeks, write affirmations, or script their goals, only to feel discouraged when results are not immediate. The missing link is not effort; it is integration. Without a way to bring these practices into real decisions, routines, and interactions, they remain isolated exercises rather than catalysts for change.

This part of the book is designed to bridge that gap. You will learn how to take the internal shifts you have cultivated and anchor them in action. Integration is not about doing more; it is about living differently — responding to challenges from alignment, seeing opportunities you once overlooked, and taking steps that feel natural rather than forced. It is where manifestation moves from theory to practice, from visualization to embodied reality.

Over the next chapters, we will explore how to recognize and act on inspired opportunities, how to create rituals that keep you connected to your vision without becoming rigid, and how to align all areas of your life — relationships, career, health — with the energy you have cultivated. By the end of this section, you will not just understand manifestation intellectually; you will have a system for living it every day.

Chapter 7 – Taking Inspired Action

The Truth About Action in Manifestation (Debunking Myths)

One of the most persistent misconceptions about manifestation is the belief that it requires no action at all — that simply thinking about what you want will cause it to appear. Popular culture has fueled this idea by reducing manifestation to positive thinking and vision boards without addressing the role of practical effort. On the other side of the spectrum, some believe manifestation demands relentless hustle, as if working harder will force the outcome into existence. Both extremes miss the truth. Real manifestation integrates internal alignment with external action, allowing results to unfold through a blend of clarity, energy, and deliberate movement.

Why Pure "Thinking" Isn't Enough

Visualization and scripting are powerful because they prime the brain to recognize opportunities and build belief, but they do not replace action. Neuroscience shows that mental rehearsal strengthens neural pathways, preparing you to act with more confidence when opportunities arise. However, without follow-through, the potential remains unrealized. Writing about abundance or picturing success creates readiness, not results. The external shift occurs when those internal changes translate into new behaviors — making the call, applying for the position, starting the conversation.

Many people who feel disillusioned with manifestation have unknowingly fallen into the trap of passive wishing. They assume that if something has not materialized, they are not visualizing hard enough, when in reality they have missed chances to act on the very alignment they were cultivating. The universe can open doors, but you must still walk through them.

The Myth of Overexertion

Equally misleading is the belief that manifestation requires constant grinding and exhaustion. In this view, success comes only through endless action, regardless of alignment. While consistent effort matters, pushing through misalignment often leads to burnout or results that do not actually feel fulfilling. Action for the sake of proving worth or forcing control rarely supports long-term change because it is driven by fear rather than trust.

Manifestation invites a different kind of action — deliberate, aligned steps that feel purposeful rather than frantic. When belief and vision are in place, action flows more naturally. Instead of exhausting yourself by doing everything at once, you begin to recognize the few steps that create meaningful progress and focus your energy there. This approach not only produces results more efficiently but also fosters a sense of ease rather than struggle.

What "Inspired Action" Really Means

Inspired action is often misunderstood as waiting for a lightning bolt of motivation. In reality, it is the willingness to respond to opportunities that arise from your alignment. These actions might be small and quiet — sending an email, following a hunch, attending an event you feel drawn to — yet they often lead to significant outcomes. The difference lies in the energy behind the action. When rooted in trust and clarity, even small steps create momentum because they align with the vision you have been cultivating.

Inspired action does not mean perfect timing or waiting until fear disappears. It means listening to intuition, acknowledging the discomfort that comes with growth, and moving forward anyway. Often, the most aligned opportunities will still feel challenging because they require you to expand beyond old patterns. The key is learning to distinguish between the discomfort of growth and the resistance that signals misalignment — a skill we will explore further in the next section.

Identifying aligned opportunities requires awareness and presence. When you are grounded in your vision, subtle cues begin to stand out — a conversation that sparks an idea, a job posting that feels like it was written for you, or a chance encounter that opens a door. These moments often go unnoticed when you are distracted or focused on rigid plans. Staying open while maintaining clarity allows you to recognize opportunities without overanalyzing or second-guessing them.

A practical way to cultivate this awareness is to check in with your emotional and physical responses when opportunities appear. Alignment is often felt in the body as calm focus or quiet excitement, even if fear arises alongside it. Misaligned choices, in contrast, usually feel heavy or constricting, accompanied by a sense of forcing rather than flowing. This distinction becomes clearer with practice, as you learn to trust the subtle signals your body gives you.

Overcoming hesitation is another essential part of inspired action. Fear rarely disappears entirely before a meaningful step; waiting for total certainty often leads to stagnation. Instead, acknowledge fear and move forward in small increments. Taking one step creates evidence that reinforces belief, which makes the next step easier. Momentum builds through action, not through waiting for perfect confidence. This approach aligns with behavioral psychology research showing that motivation often follows action rather than preceding it.

Balancing trust with practical effort is where manifestation matures into a sustainable way of living. Trust does not mean passivity, and action does not mean frantic control. It is about holding the vision lightly while continuing to show up in tangible ways. You follow through on commitments, refine your skills, and remain open to adjustments without clinging to rigid timelines. This blend of surrender and movement creates resilience because you are neither forcing outcomes nor abandoning them.

One of the most empowering realizations in manifestation is that every action you take while aligned — no matter how small — compounds over time. Sending a single email may not transform your life overnight, but combined with a steady pattern of similar steps, it creates opportunities you could not have predicted at the start. This accumulation mirrors how compound interest grows wealth: small, consistent deposits of energy and intention eventually create exponential results.

The myth that manifestation is effortless or purely mental robs people of this truth. Real manifestation is participatory. The internal work prepares you, but the external work builds the bridge between desire and reality. When you consistently show up in ways that reflect the future you are creating, your identity shifts. You stop waiting for change and start embodying it, which is ultimately what accelerates results.

By reframing action as part of alignment rather than separate from it, you dissolve the false divide between "spiritual" and "practical" effort. The two are inseparable: clarity and energy shape the quality of your actions, while your actions reinforce the beliefs and emotions you have cultivated. This is the cycle that sustains manifestation beyond initial bursts of motivation, turning it into a way of life rather than a temporary experiment.

How to Recognize "Inspired" Opportunities vs. Forced Effort

One of the biggest challenges in manifestation is discerning when to act and when to wait. Opportunities will arise, but not every option in front of you will lead to alignment. Some actions are fueled by inspiration and flow naturally from the vision you have cultivated; others are driven by fear, pressure, or the need to control outcomes. Understanding the difference is essential because the quality of your action determines not only the results you create but also the experience of getting there.

What Inspired Opportunities Feel Like

Inspired opportunities often appear subtly. They may not arrive with dramatic signs or overwhelming certainty, but they carry a sense of resonance. You might feel an inner nudge to explore something, a quiet pull toward a conversation, or a sudden clarity about the next step to take. These signals are usually accompanied by calm focus or curiosity rather than frantic urgency. Even if fear arises — which is natural when stretching beyond your comfort zone — there is an underlying sense of rightness that feels different from the anxiety of forcing something to happen.

A key characteristic of inspired action is alignment between desire and readiness. The opportunity matches the vision you have been cultivating internally, and even if it challenges you, it does not contradict your values or long-term goals. For example, if you have been visualizing meaningful work, an inspired opportunity might appear as a job posting that excites you even if it feels slightly beyond your current skill level. The stretch feels motivating rather than draining.

Signs of Forced Effort

Forced effort, on the other hand, often feels heavy or constricted. It is driven by a belief that if you do not act immediately, everything will fall apart. This energy usually comes from fear — fear of missing out, fear of lack, fear of falling behind. When action is forced, it tends to be accompanied by tension in the body, mental overthinking, and a sense of pushing rather than flowing.

Another indicator of forced effort is misalignment between the action and your deeper desires. You may pursue something because it looks good on paper, because others expect it, or because you feel pressure to prove yourself. Yet deep down, there is little excitement or connection. The result is often burnout or disappointment, even if the action technically "works." In manifestation, the path matters as much as the outcome; if the process feels draining, it is often a sign that you are acting out of alignment.

The Role of Intuition and Self-Trust

Distinguishing between inspired and forced action requires self-awareness and trust. Intuition rarely shouts; it communicates through subtle sensations, small pulls, and quiet knowing. The more you practice tuning into your body and emotions, the easier it becomes to recognize these signals. For some, inspiration feels like lightness in the chest; for others, it is a calm certainty in the gut. Learning your own cues is key to discerning next steps.

Testing alignment can be as simple as pausing before making a decision and asking yourself how the opportunity feels in your body. If there is a sense of expansion — curiosity, excitement, or openness — it is often a sign of inspiration. If the feeling is constriction, tightness, or an urgent need to prove something, that may point to forced action. This pause interrupts automatic reactions and creates space for clarity to emerge rather than letting fear dictate your next step.

Journaling can be another powerful tool to clarify whether an action is inspired. Writing out why you feel drawn to an opportunity helps surface hidden motivations. Are you acting from genuine alignment with your vision, or are you responding to fear of missing out or pressure to conform? Honest reflection often reveals the answer. Over time, this practice strengthens self-trust by showing you patterns in your choices — how you feel before inspired steps versus forced ones and the results each type of action tends to bring.

Fear deserves special attention in this process because it can easily be misread. Inspired action often carries fear, but it is the fear of expansion — stepping into something new and meaningful. Forced action carries fear of failure or scarcity, which feels heavier and more urgent. Asking yourself, "Is this fear pulling me forward or holding me back?" helps separate the discomfort of growth from the warning signs of misalignment. This distinction allows you to act despite fear when the underlying energy is right, rather than avoiding valuable opportunities simply because they feel challenging.

Building confidence in recognizing inspiration comes through practice rather than perfection. The more you experiment with small decisions — following intuitive nudges, saying yes to opportunities that feel aligned, and observing the outcomes — the more you learn to trust your internal signals. Each time you witness a positive result from listening to intuition, even in small ways, it reinforces your ability to act decisively the next time inspiration strikes.

It is also important to give yourself permission to adjust course. Not every decision will be perfectly aligned, and that is part of the learning process. Recognizing when something no longer feels right and choosing differently is not failure; it is refinement. Manifestation is a dynamic process that evolves as you grow, and the willingness to recalibrate ensures your actions remain in harmony with your vision rather than rigidly attached to old plans. Ultimately, inspired action and forced effort feel different because of the energy behind them. Inspired opportunities create momentum that feels sustainable. Even when effort is required, there is a sense of purpose and alignment that carries you through challenges. Forced effort, by contrast, drains energy and often leads to frustration or burnout. By learning to listen to subtle cues and honoring what feels genuinely aligned, you begin to create results that not only match your desires but also feel deeply fulfilling in the process.

Building Momentum with Small, Aligned Steps

Manifestation often feels overwhelming when you view your desires as massive leaps from where you are now. The gap between current reality and future vision can seem so large that it creates paralysis rather than progress. This is why momentum is built not through giant moves but through consistent, small, aligned steps. Each step, though modest on its own, compounds over time, creating a sense of movement and reinforcing belief in your ability to create change.

Why Small Steps Work

The brain responds to progress, not perfection. Behavioral science research shows that small wins release dopamine, a neurotransmitter linked to motivation and learning. Every time you complete an aligned action — even something as simple as writing a single page, making one phone call, or taking five minutes to visualize — you reinforce a feedback loop that makes future action easier. Over time, these actions accumulate into significant shifts without the burnout that often accompanies all-or-nothing approaches.

Small steps also reduce resistance. When you aim for huge changes overnight, the subconscious can perceive the goal as unsafe or unrealistic, triggering self-sabotage. Breaking the vision into approachable actions allows your nervous system to adapt gradually. This prevents the inner pushback that arises when you try to force yourself into sudden transformation and ensures that progress feels sustainable rather than forced.

Alignment Over Busyness

Momentum does not come from doing more but from doing what aligns. Many people equate productivity with progress, filling their days with tasks that are disconnected from their deeper goals. True momentum arises when each step, no matter how small, is rooted in the vision you are creating. Aligned actions feel purposeful rather than frantic; they contribute to the larger picture without draining energy.

To identify aligned steps, begin by clarifying what moves you closer to your desired state rather than just distracting you from discomfort. For example, if your vision is financial freedom, an aligned step might be starting a savings habit or researching a skill that enhances your income potential — not obsessively refreshing your bank account or comparing yourself to others online. When actions stem from clarity, they naturally create momentum because they point toward a future you genuinely care about.

The Compounding Effect

Momentum builds exponentially because aligned actions reinforce belief. Each time you follow through, you prove to yourself that change is possible. This proof quiets doubt and creates a new internal narrative: you are someone who takes steps toward your vision consistently. Over weeks and months, this identity shift becomes as important as the results themselves. You stop waiting to "become" the person who manifests and start living as that person now, which accelerates results in every area of life.

The most effective way to stack aligned actions is by anchoring them to existing routines. Habits form more easily when they attach to something you already do daily. If you want to script each morning, pair it with drinking your first cup of coffee. If you intend to visualize at night, connect it to the moment you set your phone on the nightstand. This pairing removes decision fatigue and turns new behaviors into automatic patterns rather than tasks you have to force yourself to remember.

Momentum is also strengthened by tracking progress in ways that highlight subtle shifts. Many people abandon practices because they are looking for dramatic breakthroughs and miss the quieter evidence of change — feeling calmer in stressful situations, noticing synchronicities, or responding to setbacks with more patience than before. Keeping a record of these small wins reinforces motivation and shows you that the process is working even before tangible results appear.

Consistency matters more than intensity. It is tempting to pour energy into a burst of effort at the beginning, only to burn out when life gets busy. Sustainable progress comes from actions that feel manageable enough to continue during high and low seasons alike. Even on difficult days, doing something — however small — maintains the thread of alignment and prevents the discouragement that comes from completely disengaging. This approach honors the reality that growth is not linear while still protecting your momentum.

Self-compassion plays a critical role in maintaining consistency. Missing a step or experiencing a dip in motivation is not a sign of failure but an invitation to recommit. The most transformative shifts happen when you return to alignment quickly after a lapse rather than judging yourself for it. This mindset removes unnecessary pressure and allows momentum to be rebuilt without starting from scratch each time.

As your actions accumulate, pay attention to how your internal narrative changes. At first, the focus may be on the actions themselves — writing, visualizing, making small changes. Over time, the deeper transformation is in how you see yourself. You begin to identify as someone capable of growth, someone who follows through on what matters. This shift in identity is the engine of momentum. Once you view yourself through this lens, aligned choices feel natural rather than forced, and the gap between who you are and who you are becoming steadily closes.

Momentum eventually creates a tipping point where results begin to compound more quickly. External opportunities align with your internal state, and what once felt effortful becomes second nature. The journey does not require perfection; it requires willingness to keep showing up, trusting that each small step builds toward a reality that will one day feel inevitable.

Chapter 8: Receiving Without Resistance

Why Attachment Blocks Your Manifestations

Attachment is one of the most subtle yet powerful obstacles in manifestation. It often hides behind a strong desire for change, making it difficult to recognize. On the surface, attachment looks like focus and commitment — repeating affirmations, checking for signs, obsessively thinking about the goal. But beneath this energy is fear: fear of not receiving, fear of being disappointed, fear of staying stuck. That fear tightens your grip on the outcome and creates resistance that pushes the manifestation further away.

The Energy of Attachment

Manifestation operates on alignment, not desperation. When your desire is infused with trust, you create space for opportunities to flow naturally toward you. Attachment, however, signals to your subconscious and to your nervous system that the desired outcome is the only path to happiness. This energy communicates lack rather than abundance, sending a mixed message: you say you want something, but every thought about it reinforces that you do not have it.

This is why attachment feels heavy. Instead of enjoying the vision, you feel anxious about when and how it will arrive. Instead of acting from inspiration, you second-guess every step and search constantly for proof that progress is happening. The fixation on timing and results shifts focus away from alignment and toward control, which disrupts the natural unfolding of the process.

Why Letting Go Matters

Letting go does not mean giving up on your desire. It means releasing the fear that nothing will work unless it happens exactly as you picture it. True detachment is about trusting that your vision will manifest in the right way and at the right time — sometimes in ways you could not have predicted. When you loosen the grip on how it must unfold, you create space for solutions and opportunities that may be better than what you originally imagined.

This is not just a spiritual principle; psychology supports it. Studies on goal pursuit show that excessive fixation on outcomes often leads to stress and diminished performance. People who hold their goals lightly while staying committed to aligned actions experience greater resilience and are more likely to notice opportunities along the way. The mindset shift from "I must have this now" to "I am open to this or something even better" can transform the entire process.

Attachment and Self-Worth

Attachment also reveals deeper patterns of self-worth. When your sense of value is tied to achieving a specific outcome, you unconsciously tell yourself that you are incomplete until it arrives. This creates emotional volatility — elation when things seem to move forward, despair when they do not. The cycle becomes exhausting and reinforces the very lack you are trying to overcome.

Cultivating worthiness independent of outcomes is key. When you know you are whole regardless of external circumstances, desires shift from being desperate needs to expressions of expansion. You want them, but you do not depend on them for your sense of self. This freedom dissolves resistance and allows manifestations to arrive more easily, often faster than when you were grasping tightly.

Releasing attachment begins with recognizing where it shows up in your daily habits and thoughts. Notice how often you check for evidence of progress, replay conversations in your mind, or obsessively plan each step toward your goal. These behaviors often feel productive but are actually signals of mistrust. Simply becoming aware of them softens their grip and creates space for a different response.

A practical way to shift out of attachment is to redirect focus from the outcome to the present moment. Instead of constantly asking when the manifestation will arrive, turn your attention to how you can embody the qualities of your desired reality now. If you are manifesting abundance, practice generosity with what you already have. If you are calling in love, nurture self-respect and connection in your current relationships. This approach transforms waiting into preparation and allows you to live from alignment rather than longing.

Gratitude plays a central role in releasing attachment. By appreciating what already exists, you signal abundance rather than lack. Gratitude changes the nervous system's state, calming the stress that arises when you fixate on unmet desires. A daily gratitude practice, even if brief, helps maintain perspective and reminds you that fulfillment is not postponed until after the manifestation arrives.

Another powerful technique is reframing desire with openness. When you shift from "I must have this exact thing" to "I am open to this or something even better," you release pressure without abandoning your vision. This mindset invites possibilities you may not have considered and prevents tunnel vision that blocks opportunities. It also creates resilience because you are no longer emotionally tied to one specific outcome or timeline.

Detachment is strengthened by cultivating trust — trust in yourself, in the process, and in timing. Trust develops through evidence: noticing synchronicities, reflecting on past manifestations, and remembering how previous challenges eventually worked out. Keeping a journal of these moments reinforces the belief that things unfold even when you cannot see immediate proof. Over time, this record becomes a resource you can return to whenever doubt arises.

It is equally important to address the deeper fear that fuels attachment. Often, this fear is rooted in a belief that you cannot handle life without the desired outcome. Consciously challenging that belief restores personal power. Remind yourself that while your desires are valid and worth pursuing, your worth and stability do not depend on them. This perspective paradoxically accelerates manifestation because it replaces desperation with steadiness.

Letting go does not mean passivity; it means creating from a place of freedom rather than tension. You continue taking aligned actions, visualizing, and affirming your vision, but you do so with ease rather than urgency. This energetic shift is subtle yet profound — it is the difference between gripping tightly and opening your hands to receive. When you embody this openness, manifestations often arrive more quickly and feel more satisfying, because they meet you in a state of wholeness rather than need.

Shifting into Trust and Non-Resistance

Trust is one of the most overlooked components of manifestation. Many people focus on visualizing or affirming what they want yet remain caught in cycles of control and worry. They do not realize that this inner tension creates resistance, blocking the very outcomes they are working toward. Trust, by contrast, allows energy to move freely. It creates the conditions where opportunities can unfold naturally, often in ways far better than the limited plans we try to impose.

Understanding Non-Resistance

Non-resistance does not mean passivity or indifference. It is the willingness to stop fighting what is and allow life to flow without constant mental struggle. Resistance happens when we insist that things must look a certain way or arrive on a specific timeline. This tight grip creates stress, which narrows perception and blinds us to alternate paths that may be more aligned.

Practicing non-resistance is about softening this grip. It does not mean abandoning your desires; it means loosening the attachment to how they must arrive. By releasing the need to control every detail, you invite the process to unfold in its own timing. This openness not only reduces stress but also helps you notice subtle signs, synchronicities, and opportunities you might otherwise dismiss.

Why Trust Accelerates Manifestation

Trust shifts your nervous system from survival mode into a state of receptivity. When you believe that what you desire is on its way, you stop scanning for danger or obsessively looking for proof. This calm presence allows you to think clearly, recognize opportunities, and respond to life from alignment rather than fear. Trust is not blind hope; it is a choice to align your energy with the belief that you are supported, even when you cannot see immediate results.

Research on optimism and resilience supports this principle. People who trust the process of their goals — rather than fixating on control — tend to experience greater creativity and persistence. They interpret setbacks as temporary rather than permanent and are more willing to adapt when circumstances shift. In manifestation, this mindset allows you to remain aligned even when results take time to appear.

Recognizing Resistance in Daily Life

The first step in shifting into trust is noticing where resistance shows up. It often hides in subtle behaviors: checking your phone for messages every few minutes, replaying worries in your mind, or micromanaging details to force outcomes. These actions signal to the subconscious that you doubt the process. Awareness of these patterns allows you to pause and choose a different response rather than falling into automatic control.

Pay attention to your physical cues as well. Resistance often manifests as tightness in the chest, shallow breathing, or restlessness. Trust, on the other hand, feels expansive and grounded. Learning to recognize these bodily signals helps you shift states more quickly, moving from tension into openness.

Cultivating trust begins with deliberately shifting focus from what you cannot control to what you can. Instead of obsessing over timing or outcomes, place energy on staying aligned with your vision and taking the next clear step. This shift anchors you in the present, where you can influence your state of being and actions, rather than spiraling into anxiety about the future.

One effective way to embody trust is through daily practices that reinforce the belief that you are supported. This could involve beginning each morning by affirming that everything is unfolding for your highest good or journaling about previous times when unexpected solutions appeared. Reflecting on personal experiences where challenges resolved or opportunities emerged without forced control reminds the mind that uncertainty often hides hidden blessings.

Breathwork can also help release resistance in real time. When you catch yourself clenching around a desired outcome, pause and take slow, intentional breaths. Imagine exhaling tension and inhaling openness. This physical act calms the nervous system and signals safety, allowing your energy to shift from constriction to receptivity. Over time, this practice conditions your body to recognize that trust is not passive but active — a conscious relaxation into the process.

Reframing setbacks is equally important. Moments that appear as delays or failures often carry insights that refine your vision. Viewing them as part of the unfolding rather than as signs of defeat preserves alignment. Ask yourself, "What is this teaching me?" or "How could this redirect me toward something even better?" These questions transform resistance into curiosity, which softens fear and restores a sense of possibility.

Another layer of trust involves embracing flexibility in how your desires manifest. The outcome may arrive through an unexpected path — a conversation that leads to an opportunity you never planned for or a door closing that guides you toward something better. Holding space for possibilities beyond your current imagination removes unnecessary limits and allows life to surprise you. This openness does not dilute your vision; it expands it.

Trust deepens as you build evidence of alignment. Each time you follow an intuitive nudge and witness a positive result, even in small ways, your confidence grows. This reinforces a cycle where trusting leads to action, which leads to results, which further strengthens trust. Over months and years, this becomes a way of living rather than a technique you have to remember.

Ultimately, shifting into trust and non-resistance transforms manifestation from a struggle into a collaboration with life. You remain committed to your vision while releasing the need to control every detail. This balance allows manifestations to arrive in ways that feel effortless yet deeply aligned. When you no longer resist the process, you create space for outcomes that often exceed what you originally imagined, because you are open to receiving without fear or limitation.

Gratitude Practices that Open the Flow of Receiving

Gratitude is more than a polite acknowledgment of blessings; it is one of the most transformative states you can cultivate when manifesting. When you are grateful, you shift your attention from lack to abundance, which directly influences how your mind and body perceive the world. This shift has measurable effects. Neuroscientific studies show that gratitude activates brain regions associated with motivation and reward, releasing dopamine and serotonin that reinforce positive emotional states. In the context of manifestation, this means gratitude not only feels good but actively primes you to receive more of what you appreciate.

Why Gratitude Unlocks Receiving

Manifestation depends on alignment. When you focus on what is missing, your energy communicates scarcity. Gratitude reverses this by signaling that abundance is already present, even in small forms. This energy creates openness rather than grasping, allowing more opportunities to flow toward you. It also builds trust, reminding you that life is already working in your favor in ways you may not always notice.

Gratitude strengthens emotional resilience as well. During challenges, it grounds you in what is still working, preventing you from being consumed by what is not. This balanced perspective keeps you receptive to solutions and insights that might otherwise be overlooked when you are caught in frustration or fear.

Daily Gratitude Rituals

Creating a daily gratitude practice does not require elaborate routines. The most effective methods are simple and consistent, woven into your existing day. One powerful approach is journaling three to five things you are grateful for each morning. The key is specificity — rather than writing "I'm grateful for my family," you might write "I'm grateful for the way my sister called yesterday and listened when I felt stressed." Specific details make the practice more emotionally impactful, which strengthens its effects on the brain.

Evening reflection is another option. Before bed, review moments from the day that brought a sense of joy or relief, no matter how small. This trains your mind to seek positive experiences during the day, knowing it will be asked to recall them later. Over time, you begin to notice more reasons for gratitude in real time, not just in reflection.

Gratitude in Real Time

Beyond structured rituals, spontaneous gratitude throughout the day is equally powerful. Pausing to silently appreciate a warm cup of coffee, a kind gesture, or a moment of peace interrupts negative thought patterns and re-centers your energy. These micro-moments of gratitude accumulate, creating a baseline of appreciation that supports manifestation without requiring extra effort.

Gratitude can also be directed toward what has not yet manifested. This may feel counterintuitive at first, but expressing thanks for a desire as if it is already yours bridges the gap between vision and reality. It conditions your subconscious to treat the manifestation as inevitable, which influences your emotions and behaviors in subtle but significant ways.

Advanced gratitude practices deepen the emotional intensity behind appreciation, making it more than an intellectual exercise. One method is embodied gratitude, where you intentionally involve the senses and body. Instead of simply listing what you are thankful for, close your eyes and feel the sensation of gratitude expanding through your chest. Imagine warmth radiating outward as you think of something meaningful. This physical anchoring strengthens the neural pathways associated with positive emotion, making gratitude easier to access in daily life.

Future pacing is another powerful technique. It involves imagining yourself already living in the reality you are manifesting and expressing gratitude from that future perspective. You might visualize waking up in your dream home, feeling the textures of the space, and silently thanking life for supporting you in getting there. This practice merges visualization with gratitude, aligning emotions and beliefs with the desired outcome while bypassing the sense of lack that often comes from waiting.

Gratitude can also be extended toward challenges, which transforms how you respond to difficulties. When you can acknowledge the growth, lessons, or strength gained from a struggle, you neutralize resistance and open yourself to unexpected blessings. For example, feeling grateful for the patience developed during a financial setback reframes the situation from limitation to preparation. This shift softens negative energy and allows solutions to emerge more easily.

Combining gratitude with other manifestation tools enhances its effect. Writing scripts infused with appreciation — thanking life for what you desire as though it is already present — blends the power of narrative with emotional alignment. Meditations focused on gratitude can also be layered with breathwork, where each inhale welcomes abundance and each exhale releases tension. These integrations make gratitude a dynamic force rather than a standalone practice.

Consistency is more impactful than intensity. It is better to cultivate small, regular moments of appreciation than to attempt occasional, elaborate gratitude sessions. Over time, this steady practice rewires your default perspective toward abundance, which influences how you interpret experiences and interact with opportunities. The shift is subtle but cumulative, leading to noticeable changes in mood, outlook, and openness to receiving.

Tracking the ripple effects of gratitude reinforces motivation to continue. As you notice synchronicities, improved relationships, or a calmer emotional baseline, record them in a journal. These observations build evidence that the practice is working, which strengthens belief and creates a feedback loop. The more you acknowledge what is unfolding, the more attuned you become to noticing blessings you might have missed before.

Ultimately, gratitude is both a bridge and a magnet. It bridges the gap between where you are and where you want to be by aligning your energy with fulfillment rather than longing. At the same time, it magnetizes opportunities by shifting focus toward what is already abundant, inviting more of it into your life. When practiced deeply and consistently, gratitude becomes not just a tool for manifestation but a way of experiencing life that transforms every stage of the journey.

Chapter 9: Building Daily Manifestation Rituals

Morning Practices That Prime Your Energy for the Day

How you begin your morning sets the tone for everything that follows. The first moments after waking are when your subconscious mind is most receptive, making them a powerful window for aligning thoughts, emotions, and energy with the life you are creating. Many people start the day on autopilot — scrolling their phones, rushing into tasks, and absorbing stress before their minds have a chance to orient toward what matters. Reclaiming these moments transforms the rest of the day, allowing you to respond intentionally rather than react impulsively.

The Science of Morning Energy

Your brain cycles through different states as you transition from sleep to wakefulness. In the first 20 to 30 minutes, brainwave activity remains in alpha and theta frequencies, the same states accessed during meditation and deep visualization. This makes it easier to imprint new beliefs, strengthen affirmations, and set emotional tone for the day ahead. When you use this window to focus on alignment rather than chaos, you influence not only your mood but also your perception of opportunities and challenges throughout the day.

Morning routines also stabilize the nervous system. A calm, intentional start regulates cortisol levels — the stress hormone that spikes naturally upon waking — and prevents that spike from tipping into anxiety. This foundation of physiological calm improves focus, decision-making, and emotional resilience, all of which are essential for maintaining alignment during real-life challenges.

Creating a Grounded Start

The goal of a morning practice is not to create a rigid checklist but to establish a framework that grounds and energizes you. Even five to ten minutes of intentional focus can shift your state. The key is to prioritize practices that connect you to your vision and prime your energy rather than overwhelm you with complexity.

Start by creating space for quiet before external demands intrude. Avoid immediately checking notifications or diving into responsibilities. Instead, give yourself a brief moment to orient inward: How do you want to feel today? What qualities do you want to embody? This pause alone begins to shift your energy from reactivity to intention.

Breath and Movement

Simple breathwork is one of the fastest ways to activate presence in the morning. A few cycles of slow, deep breathing oxygenate the body, calm lingering tension from sleep, and bring focus to the present moment. Pairing breath with gentle movement — stretching, standing tall, rolling the shoulders — helps awaken circulation and signals to the body that it is time to engage fully with the day.

This mindful movement is not about burning calories or following strict exercise regimens. It is about reconnecting with your body, shaking off the heaviness of sleep, and inviting a sense of vitality. When the body feels open and energized, the mind follows, making it easier to hold the emotional state that supports manifestation.

Layering visualization into your morning amplifies the energy created through breath and movement. Once the body feels awake, close your eyes and picture yourself living a typical day in the reality you are manifesting. Rather than imagining distant goals in abstract terms, focus on the details of what life feels like once those desires have already arrived. See yourself interacting confidently, moving through spaces that reflect abundance, and feeling gratitude as if it were already present. The more sensory-rich the visualization, the stronger the signal it sends to your subconscious mind.

Pairing this visualization with gratitude magnifies its effect. As you picture your desired reality, express silent thanks for it as if it exists now. This practice bridges the emotional gap between where you are and where you want to be, aligning your nervous system with the state of receiving rather than longing. Gratitude softens any tension around timing and primes you to notice opportunities that align with what you are calling in.

Morning practices are also the ideal time for intentional self-talk. Affirmations work best when they feel believable and emotionally resonant.

Choose statements that reflect your desired identity rather than forced positivity. For example, instead of saying "I am rich," you might affirm "I am learning to manage money wisely and create abundance daily." These nuanced statements bypass inner resistance while still guiding your mind toward growth. Repeating them aloud or writing them down engages multiple senses, deepening their impact.

Incorporating mindful planning ensures your morning practice extends into tangible action. Rather than overwhelming yourself with an exhaustive to-do list, identify one to three key actions that feel aligned with your larger vision. These are not simply tasks for the sake of productivity but intentional steps that move you closer to what you are manifesting. When your plan for the day flows from a grounded state, the energy behind each action is focused and purposeful rather than scattered.

Consistency matters more than length or complexity. A five-minute routine practiced daily will create more profound shifts than an hour-long practice you cannot sustain. Allow the structure to evolve with your needs rather than forcing yourself into rigid habits. Some mornings might emphasize stillness and reflection, while others lean toward movement and affirmation. The flexibility prevents the practice from becoming another source of pressure and keeps it aligned with your natural rhythms.

Over time, the benefits compound. You begin to notice greater emotional stability, quicker recovery from stress, and a heightened awareness of synchronicities throughout the day. Challenges feel less overwhelming because you have already anchored your state before they appear. This steady internal alignment turns mornings from a chaotic scramble into a foundation for intentional living, where each day begins with clarity and ends with a sense of progress.

Evening Reflections That Lock in Progress Overnight

The way you close your day is just as important as how you begin it. Evenings provide a natural moment to consolidate progress, release tension, and prepare the subconscious mind for integration during sleep. While mornings set intention, nights are for reflection — a quiet reckoning with how you lived your day and what energy you carry forward. This reflective process strengthens the manifestation cycle by ensuring that every experience, even the challenging ones, contributes to your alignment.

Why Evenings Hold Transformative Power

Sleep is not simply rest; it is a time when the brain processes memories, consolidates learning, and reorganizes emotional experiences. What you focus on before sleeping directly influences this process. Dwelling on stress or replaying negative moments reinforces them in the subconscious, while intentional reflection and gratitude help imprint positive patterns instead. Over time, this shapes not only your mood upon waking but also your default mindset and receptivity to manifestation.

Evening practices create closure. Without them, unresolved energy lingers overnight, feeding restlessness or anxiety. Reflection acts as a reset, allowing you to end the day with a sense of completion rather than carrying yesterday's weight into tomorrow. This sense of closure signals safety to the nervous system, which supports deeper sleep and primes the mind to integrate affirmations or visualizations more effectively.

Acknowledging the Day Without Judgment

The first step in evening reflection is reviewing your day with honesty rather than criticism. Ask yourself: How did I show up? Where did I align with my vision? Where did I drift? The goal is not to grade your performance but to observe patterns. This compassionate awareness prevents shame and encourages curiosity, which fosters growth. It also builds self-trust by showing that you are willing to look at your life directly rather than avoiding discomfort.

A helpful approach is to note both moments of alignment and areas for adjustment. For example, you might recognize a conversation where you responded with patience or an instance where you reverted to old habits. Seeing both sides balances your perspective. You are neither glorifying the positive nor dwelling on the negative; you are collecting data to inform tomorrow's intentions.

Releasing Emotional Residue

Reflection is incomplete without releasing the emotional residue of the day. Lingering frustration, disappointment, or even overstimulation can carry into sleep and influence how you feel in the morning. Simple techniques like deep breathing, gentle stretching, or writing a few sentences about what you are letting go can clear this energetic clutter. The act of releasing is less about solving problems and more about setting them down for the night, trusting that clarity will come with rest.

Integrating gratitude into your nightly reflection amplifies the sense of closure and alignment. After acknowledging and releasing the day, take a few moments to name what you appreciate — not only the obvious wins but also the subtle gifts that might otherwise go unnoticed. This could be a conversation that shifted your mood, a moment of calm during chaos, or even the lessons hidden in challenges. Specificity matters here; the more vividly you recall these moments, the more deeply your nervous system absorbs the feeling of abundance.

Gratitude can extend into future-oriented visualization. Once you have cleared the emotional residue of the day and grounded in appreciation, gently picture the next steps you are calling in. Imagine yourself moving through tomorrow with clarity and ease, or see a bigger goal unfolding naturally over time. The key is to hold these visions lightly, without grasping. This trains your subconscious to associate your desires with calm expectancy rather than pressure, allowing sleep to become a rehearsal space for alignment.

Evening reflection also benefits from gentle intention-setting. This is not about creating a detailed plan for tomorrow but rather anchoring one guiding quality or focus. You might choose patience, creativity, or confidence — whatever feels most supportive for the next phase of your journey. Writing this intention down or speaking it aloud creates a small ritual of commitment that carries into the following day.

Journaling is an effective tool for consolidating all these elements — review, release, gratitude, and intention — in one place. The act of writing slows your thoughts, turning abstract emotions into tangible insights. Over time, this journal becomes a record of growth, showing how small daily shifts accumulate into significant transformation. Re-reading past entries can be motivating during plateaus, reminding you how far you have come even when results feel slow.

Preparing your environment for rest supports the process as much as the mental practices. Dimming lights, reducing noise, and limiting screens signal to the body that it is time to wind down. Creating a consistent bedtime ritual, even if brief, conditions your system to associate certain cues — like a cup of herbal tea or a few minutes of quiet breathing — with safety and closure. When your body feels secure, your mind can more easily integrate the reflections and intentions you have set.

The cumulative effect of evening practices is subtle but profound. Instead of carrying the weight of unresolved thoughts into sleep, you enter rest with a sense of completion and openness. Over time, this habit creates a deeper sense of self-trust. You no longer fear setbacks because you know you will meet them with awareness, release what no longer serves, and extract the lessons that propel you forward. This daily rhythm of reflection turns every night into an opportunity to lock in progress and begin anew, grounded and aligned.

Creating a Personalized Routine That Actually Sticks

Manifestation practices only transform your life when they are sustainable. A perfectly designed routine that feels inspiring on paper will not serve you if it collapses under the weight of unrealistic expectations. Many people begin with ambitious plans — an hour of meditation, journaling, exercise, and visualization every morning — only to abandon them within weeks. The key is to create a routine that adapts to your lifestyle, honors your energy, and grows with you over time.

Why Personalization Matters

No two lives are the same. Work schedules, family responsibilities, personal energy rhythms, and even creative peaks vary from person to person. A routine that works for someone who wakes up energized at 5 a.m. will not work for someone whose clarity arrives at night. Forcing yourself into practices that do not align with your natural rhythms creates resistance, which defeats the purpose of manifestation work. Personalization ensures that your routine feels supportive rather than burdensome, making it easier to stay consistent.

Personalization also acknowledges that your needs will evolve. During periods of intense growth or transition, you may crave longer practices for grounding and clarity. At other times, brief check-ins may be enough to maintain alignment. Designing your routine with built-in flexibility prevents guilt when life shifts and allows you to maintain the core essence of your practice even when circumstances change.

Start with Core Principles, Not Rigid Rules

The most effective routines are built on principles rather than strict formulas. Instead of dictating exact times or formats, focus on the underlying goals: setting intention, aligning energy, and reflecting on progress. How you achieve those goals can vary day to day. For example, intention-setting might involve scripting on one morning and silent visualization on another, depending on what feels most nourishing.

By anchoring your practice to principles, you reduce the all-or-nothing thinking that often derails routines. Missing a journaling session does not mean you have failed; it simply means you can choose another alignment practice instead. This flexibility maintains momentum and prevents the discouragement that comes from unrealistic perfectionism.

Aligning with Your Energy Patterns

An often-overlooked factor in routine design is energy mapping. Pay attention to when you naturally feel most focused, calm, or creative, and schedule manifestation practices around those windows. If mornings are hectic, forcing a 30-minute ritual may add stress rather than ease. In that case, consider a brief breathing practice in the morning paired with a deeper reflection in the evening. The goal is not to follow a trend but to honor what supports your nervous system and lifestyle.

Experimentation is essential in finding a rhythm that feels natural. Begin with a simple version of your routine rather than an idealized one. Start small — perhaps five minutes of visualization or gratitude — and allow it to expand gradually as it becomes part of your life. This approach prevents overwhelm and allows you to notice which practices feel most impactful. Pay attention to the emotional shifts you experience. The right practices leave you feeling grounded and focused rather than pressured or drained.

Refinement comes from observing your patterns over time. After a week or two, reflect on which elements you look forward to and which feel forced. The practices that resonate will naturally become anchors; those that feel heavy can be adjusted or replaced without guilt. For example, if journaling feels repetitive, try speaking affirmations aloud or recording a voice note. The purpose is not to fit into a single mold but to find what consistently reconnects you to alignment.

Integrating routines into daily life requires reducing friction. Make your chosen practices as accessible as possible. Keep your journal on the nightstand instead of in a drawer. Set reminders that prompt you to pause for a brief visualization. Arrange your space so cues for alignment are visible and inviting rather than hidden or inconvenient. Small environmental adjustments remove excuses and turn rituals into seamless extensions of your day.

Flexibility is equally important. A routine that collapses the moment you travel or face a busy schedule will not support long-term growth. Design a "minimum version" of your practice — a condensed set of actions you can do anywhere, even in a few minutes. This ensures that no matter what life throws at you, you maintain connection to your vision. Consistency comes not from rigid discipline but from adaptability grounded in intention.

As your routine solidifies, track its impact beyond the practice itself. Notice how your mood, decisions, and energy shift throughout the day. Do you respond to stress differently? Are you more aware of opportunities or intuitive nudges? Documenting these subtle changes reinforces motivation and helps you appreciate the quiet ways manifestation unfolds. This evidence also makes it easier to recommit on days when you feel disconnected, reminding you why the practice matters.

Over time, your personalized routine evolves into more than a habit; it becomes a stabilizing framework for growth. It shapes how you wake, how you reflect, and how you interact with the world. Most importantly, it grounds you in a consistent state of alignment that carries into every action you take. When your routine flows with who you are rather than against it, consistency stops being a struggle and becomes part of your identity. The result is not only a practice that sticks but one that continues to deepen as your manifestations unfold and your vision expands.

Part IV. Application & Expansion

By the time you arrive at this stage, you have built the foundation for manifestation and learned to align thoughts, emotions, and actions with what you desire. You have explored core techniques, dismantled limiting beliefs, and cultivated daily rituals that keep you grounded. Now comes the deeper work: applying these principles across every area of life and expanding beyond personal goals into something even greater.

This part is about integration. It is one thing to create moments of alignment during meditation or journaling; it is another to carry that alignment into relationships, career, health, and the unpredictable flow of everyday life. True mastery happens when your practices stop feeling separate from who you are and begin shaping how you move through the world.

Here, you will learn how to manifest not just isolated desires but a cohesive life that reflects your highest vision. Money, love, vitality, and purpose each have their own energetic patterns, and understanding how to navigate them allows manifestation to feel effortless rather than fragmented. You will also see how to handle setbacks and plateaus — the inevitable pauses that are not signs of failure but invitations to refine alignment and deepen trust.

The final chapters will guide you toward living as a receiver rather than a seeker. This shift from chasing to embodying is what transforms manifestation from a temporary practice into a permanent way of being. It is where you stop asking "How do I get there?" and begin living as though you already are. In this space, your goals expand beyond personal gain. The energy you cultivate starts to influence the people around you, inspiring connection and contributing to something larger than yourself.

As you move through these chapters, remember that expansion does not mean more striving. It means broadening the scope of your alignment, applying it in ways that bring coherence and depth to every part of your life. This is where manifestation evolves from a tool into a path — one that continues to unfold long after you finish this book.

Chapter 10: Manifesting Across Life Areas

Money and Abundance: Beyond "Think Rich"

Money is often the first area where people apply manifestation techniques. It is tangible, measurable, and tied to daily survival, which makes financial goals feel urgent. Yet this urgency is precisely what blocks abundance for many. The message of simply "thinking rich" oversimplifies a complex relationship shaped by beliefs, habits, and energy. True abundance requires more than positive thoughts; it calls for dismantling scarcity conditioning and aligning with the deeper meaning money holds in your life.

Rewriting the Money Story

Most people inherit unexamined beliefs about money from family, culture, or personal experiences. You may have heard phrases like "money doesn't grow on trees" or "rich people are greedy," which quietly shaped how you view wealth. Even subtle narratives — such as equating financial success with worthiness — can create internal conflict. If a part of you believes money is dangerous or unspiritual, no amount of affirmations will override the subconscious resistance to receiving it.

Rewriting your money story begins with awareness. Reflect on the messages you absorbed growing up and how they influence your current choices. Do you associate wealth with freedom or fear? Do you feel guilt when you desire more? Examining these patterns is not about blame but clarity. Once you identify the underlying scripts, you can begin replacing them with beliefs that support expansion rather than limitation.

Shifting from Scarcity to Sufficiency

Scarcity thinking does not always look like desperation. It can show up subtly — comparing yourself to others, hoarding resources out of fear, or believing opportunities are finite. This mindset narrows your vision and keeps you focused on what is missing rather than what is possible. Abundance, in contrast, is the recognition that resources, ideas, and opportunities can flow in many forms, often beyond what you currently imagine.

Cultivating sufficiency is a powerful bridge to abundance. It does not mean ignoring financial goals but grounding yourself in the sense that you already have enough in this moment. From that emotional baseline, you can create more without grasping. Studies in behavioral science show that people who feel abundant — even before external changes — make better decisions, take calculated risks, and attract opportunities more easily than those operating from fear.

Energy and Practicality Together

One of the biggest misconceptions about money manifestation is that it happens only in the mind. Energy matters, but so do actions, skills, and systems. True abundance integrates inner alignment with external strategy. Visualizing financial freedom can prime you emotionally, but following through with budgeting, learning new skills, or exploring additional income streams anchors that energy in the physical world. Manifestation is not magic without participation; it is a partnership between belief and behavior. A powerful shift occurs when you stop viewing wealth as a means of escape and begin seeing it as a tool for contribution. When money becomes solely about escaping fear — paying off debt, leaving an unfulfilling job, avoiding scarcity — it remains tied to survival. But when you frame wealth as a way to expand your impact, support others, and create meaningful experiences, the energy around it changes. The focus moves from anxiety to purpose, which not only attracts opportunities but also gives your financial goals deeper resonance.

Integrating this mindset into daily life involves small, consistent actions. Start by aligning financial choices with the values you want to embody. If generosity is part of your vision, practice giving even in small amounts, reinforcing the belief that there is always enough to share. If freedom is central to your goals, prioritize decisions that create spaciousness — paying down obligations, simplifying expenses, or investing in skills that increase autonomy. These micro-decisions create a feedback loop where energy and action support each other, steadily building a new financial reality.

Practices like money gratitude journaling can reinforce this shift. Acknowledge every inflow, no matter how small — a paycheck, a refund, even unexpected discounts. This trains your mind to notice abundance rather than absence and conditions you to expect more of it. Coupled with visualization, where you picture yourself confidently managing and enjoying wealth, these practices rewire both belief and behavior. Neuroscience research shows that repeated mental rehearsal combined with action strengthens neural pathways, making new financial habits more automatic over time.

Another crucial element is learning to detach worth from net worth. Many people unconsciously link self-esteem to their financial status, leading to cycles of shame when they are not "where they should be." This attachment creates resistance and keeps abundance at arm's length. When you begin affirming worthiness regardless of current numbers, money can flow without the weight of proving yourself through it. You stop chasing validation and start attracting aligned opportunities because your energy is rooted in stability rather than lack.

Finally, building abundance requires patience. Financial transformation rarely happens overnight, and that is not a flaw in the process. The slow accumulation of small wins — consistent saving, saying yes to new opportunities, learning to invest — compounds over months and years. Trusting this process allows you to celebrate progress rather than constantly measuring the distance to the finish line. Each aligned step is both a result and a signal that more is on the way.

When you approach money as an extension of your values rather than as an isolated goal, manifestation becomes far more sustainable. You are not just "thinking rich"; you are living richly — grounded, purposeful, and open to receiving more than you once thought possible. This alignment of energy and action creates not only financial growth but also a sense of freedom that expands into every other area of your life.

Love and Relationships: Aligning Energy with Connection

Manifestation in love and relationships often stirs the deepest emotions. Few areas of life expose desires and fears as intensely as the longing for meaningful connection. Many people approach this area with mixed energy — craving closeness while carrying wounds from past experiences. True alignment in relationships begins not with finding the right person but with becoming the version of yourself who naturally attracts and sustains the love you seek.

The Energy You Bring

Relationships mirror the energy you hold. If you approach love from fear of abandonment, resentment, or unworthiness, you unconsciously project those patterns onto potential partners. This is not about blaming yourself for past dynamics but recognizing that energy sets the tone for connection. When you align with a sense of wholeness, you stop seeking someone to complete you and instead invite someone to share what you have already cultivated within.

This shift changes how you show up in every interaction. Rather than performing or over-giving to earn affection, you express authenticity. Rather than clinging to incompatible connections out of fear of being alone, you trust that letting go creates space for alignment. The goal is not perfection but congruence — living in a way that reflects the love you hope to receive.

Healing Before Attracting

One of the most overlooked steps in manifesting love is addressing unresolved wounds. Past betrayals, unhealed breakups, or childhood patterns of neglect often linger as subconscious blocks. Without conscious attention, these experiences shape beliefs like "love always ends" or "I am too much." Such narratives distort perception, causing you to misinterpret genuine affection or settle for dynamics that reinforce old pain.

Healing begins with awareness. Reflect on recurring themes in past relationships: the kinds of partners you are drawn to, the conflicts that arise, and the emotional responses they trigger. These patterns are not coincidences; they are invitations to examine deeper needs. Practices like journaling, therapy, or guided self-reflection help bring these patterns into the light, where they can be reworked rather than repeated.

Cultivating Self-Connection

Alignment in love is grounded in self-connection. When you know your values, boundaries, and desires, you naturally filter out relationships that do not serve you. Self-connection also fuels emotional regulation; you are less reactive to triggers because you can soothe yourself rather than relying on someone else to fill the void.

A simple yet profound practice is asking yourself daily, "How do I want to feel in love, and how can I cultivate that feeling now?" If you desire respect, treat yourself with respect in your routines and choices. If you long for passion, pursue activities that ignite joy and creativity. By embodying the emotional qualities you want from a partner, you send a consistent signal that draws matching energy into your life.

Practical alignment begins with clarifying what kind of relationship you genuinely desire rather than what you think you should want. Many people unconsciously adopt ideals from family, culture, or social media without questioning whether those dynamics feel fulfilling. Writing out the emotional qualities you seek — safety, playfulness, mutual respect — offers a compass far more reliable than a checklist of superficial traits. This clarity becomes the foundation for both attracting new connections and improving existing ones.

Visualization deepens this process by rehearsing the feeling of connection before it arrives. Rather than picturing a specific person, focus on the emotional experience: laughing with someone who understands you, feeling safe to share your truth, celebrating milestones together. Imagining these moments in sensory detail conditions your nervous system to recognize and welcome real-life opportunities that match those feelings. It also softens anxiety by signaling that love is possible and already unfolding.

Clearing resistance is equally important. Even as you envision healthy love, part of you may brace for disappointment. This protective reflex can show up as distrust, hyper-independence, or overanalyzing every interaction. Addressing these tendencies with compassion — acknowledging why they developed and choosing new responses — allows intimacy to grow without constant self-sabotage. It is not about erasing fear completely but learning to move forward even while it exists.

For those already in relationships, alignment is about deepening connection rather than starting over. This often requires shifting from expecting a partner to meet every need to co-creating a dynamic where both people take responsibility for their energy. Practices like intentional check-ins, shared gratitude rituals, or simply listening without rushing to fix can transform communication. When both partners approach the relationship as collaborators rather than adversaries, conflicts become opportunities for growth rather than threats to connection.

Boundaries are another essential aspect of aligned love. They are not walls but frameworks that protect authenticity. Clear boundaries prevent resentment and invite mutual respect. Expressing needs without blame — "I feel connected when we spend uninterrupted time together" rather than "You never pay attention to me" — fosters openness and trust. Healthy boundaries create safety, which paradoxically allows deeper vulnerability.

Love aligned with manifestation is not about perfect harmony at all times. It is about two evolving individuals choosing alignment repeatedly, even when imperfections arise. This perspective removes pressure and replaces it with curiosity: How can we grow closer through this challenge? What is this moment teaching me about my own patterns? By approaching love as a shared journey rather than a fixed destination, you create space for the relationship to expand beyond initial expectations.

Ultimately, aligning energy with connection shifts the narrative of love from scarcity to abundance. You stop searching for someone to complete you and instead invite relationships that reflect your wholeness. Whether single or partnered, this approach transforms how you give and receive love — not as a desperate pursuit but as a natural extension of the life you are already building.

Health and Vitality: Integrating Mind-Body Practices

Health is one of the clearest reflections of how aligned you are with yourself. When energy is scattered, stress unprocessed, or beliefs about the body are rooted in fear, vitality suffers. True wellness is not just the absence of illness but the presence of balance — a state where the mind, emotions, and physical body work together rather than against each other. Integrating manifestation into health is not about bypassing medical care but about creating an inner environment where healing and resilience naturally thrive.

The Mind-Body Connection

Science continues to validate what ancient traditions have long understood: the mind and body are inseparable. Thoughts and emotions influence everything from hormone regulation to immune function. Chronic stress, for example, triggers the release of cortisol, which over time disrupts sleep, digestion, and even weight balance. Conversely, practices that cultivate calm and positive expectancy can reduce inflammation, improve cardiovascular health, and enhance recovery from illness.

Recognizing this connection is empowering. It reframes health not as something dictated solely by genetics or external circumstances but as a dynamic relationship you can influence daily. While you cannot control every factor, you can shift how your nervous system responds to stress, how your thoughts shape habits, and how your emotional state supports or hinders healing.

Energy Alignment and the Body

Manifestation in the realm of health begins with the energy you bring to your own body. Many people approach wellness from criticism — focusing on what is wrong, what they dislike, or what they fear might happen. This constant focus on deficits creates tension and often fuels the very habits they wish to change. Alignment means approaching the body with respect and curiosity rather than punishment.

Start by observing the language you use when thinking about your health. Are you telling yourself you are broken or behind? Or do you affirm your body's ability to adapt and recover? Shifting this inner dialogue is not about denying challenges but about creating a supportive internal climate where healing feels possible rather than hopeless.

Integrating Simple Practices

Mind-body alignment does not require extreme routines. In fact, sustainable practices are often simple: mindful breathing to calm the nervous system, gentle movement to release stagnant energy, or short gratitude reflections focused on what the body allows you to do rather than what it cannot. These practices reinforce safety and connection, both of which are prerequisites for deeper healing.

Movement, in particular, is a potent manifestation tool. Activities like walking, yoga, or stretching do more than strengthen muscles; they regulate mood, improve circulation, and create a sense of presence. When combined with intentional thought — affirming vitality during movement rather than counting flaws — the impact compounds, transforming exercise from obligation to celebration.

Daily rituals work best when they anchor you into presence rather than add another layer of pressure. One effective approach is to begin and end the day with brief check-ins. In the morning, ask yourself how you want to feel physically and emotionally. In the evening, notice what supported or drained your energy throughout the day. These moments of awareness guide adjustments naturally rather than forcing drastic changes. Over time, they help you understand what truly nourishes you.

Reframing nourishment itself is central to manifesting vitality. Instead of obsessing over restriction or labeling foods as "good" or "bad," view what you eat as energy you are choosing to invite into your body. This perspective creates a positive relationship with nourishment rather than one built on guilt. When you eat with mindfulness — noticing textures, flavors, and how your body responds — you shift from autopilot consumption to intentional care.

Hydration, sleep, and restorative rest often play a larger role in manifestation than people realize. Lack of sleep heightens stress hormones and reduces your capacity to focus, making alignment harder to sustain. Consistently choosing rest is an act of trust: you allow the body time to repair and integrate rather than pushing through exhaustion. Prioritizing these basics may feel unglamorous, but they create the stable foundation from which higher-level practices become far more effective.

Visualization techniques can also support healing and vitality. Imagine energy flowing through areas of tension or envision your body performing at its best. Athletes and recovery patients have long used mental rehearsal to enhance physical outcomes, and the same principle applies here. When you repeatedly picture health rather than illness, your body begins responding to that expectation, influencing hormones, neural pathways, and even immune responses.

Equally important is learning to interpret the body's signals without judgment. Fatigue, tension, or discomfort are not punishments but communication. Instead of fighting these sensations, approach them with curiosity: What is my body asking for? Do I need rest, movement, nourishment, or emotional release? This dialogue transforms the body from an obstacle into an ally.

Creating vitality through mind-body practices is not about chasing perfection but cultivating resilience. There will be days when stress, illness, or old habits resurface. The goal is not to eliminate every fluctuation but to recover alignment more quickly each time. Over months and years, this resilience becomes your baseline. Your body learns that it is safe to thrive, and your mind trusts the process rather than resisting every setback.

When health and manifestation work in harmony, energy is no longer something you fight for — it flows naturally from how you live. You begin to see your body not as separate from your goals but as the vehicle through which they are realized. This integration turns wellness into a byproduct of alignment, allowing you to create and receive not just wealth or love but a life that feels vibrant at every level.

Chapter 11: Overcoming Setbacks and Plateaus

Why Manifestations Sometimes Stall (and What to Do About It)

Few experiences in manifestation feel as discouraging as waiting for a desire that seems stuck. You have done the visualizations, repeated affirmations, and followed the steps, yet nothing seems to change. This stagnation can create doubt — not only in the process but in yourself. Understanding why manifestations sometimes appear to stall is essential, because these moments are rarely failures. They are signals pointing toward deeper alignment, unrecognized resistance, or timing that serves your growth in ways you cannot yet see.

Unseen Resistance

The most common reason manifestations stall is subconscious resistance. On a surface level, you may want something wholeheartedly, but deeper beliefs can quietly contradict that desire. For example, someone might affirm financial abundance while holding unexamined fears about judgment from family or discomfort with visibility. These hidden narratives create an energetic push-pull: consciously calling something in while unconsciously keeping it at a distance.

Becoming aware of this resistance requires honest reflection. Ask yourself what fears arise when you imagine the desire fully realized. What might you have to release or change about your identity to receive it? Often, the very growth required to sustain the manifestation is what feels uncomfortable. Recognizing this discomfort does not mean abandoning the goal but addressing the layers beneath it so your energy becomes congruent rather than divided.

Misalignment Between Vision and Action

Another reason for perceived stagnation is the gap between inner alignment and outer behavior. Visualization and belief are powerful, but they work best when paired with choices that reinforce the vision. If you are manifesting better health yet consistently neglect sleep or nutrition, your body receives mixed signals. Similarly, calling in financial abundance while avoiding opportunities to learn new skills or manage resources can slow results.

This is not about forcing action from fear but about ensuring your behavior reflects the reality you are creating. Small, consistent steps — saving a small amount, speaking honestly in relationships, prioritizing rest — send a message to the subconscious that the vision is already in motion. Over time, these aligned actions bridge the gap between where you are and where you want to be.

The Role of Timing

Manifestation is not always immediate because timing is part of the process. Some desires require external elements to align — opportunities, people, or circumstances beyond your direct control. These delays can feel frustrating, yet they often serve a purpose. Sometimes the pause allows you to develop qualities or resilience that prepare you for what is coming. Other times it creates space for something even better than your original vision.

Learning to trust timing does not mean passively waiting; it means staying present, continuing aligned actions, and releasing the anxiety that pushes outcomes away. Patience combined with steady focus allows manifestations to arrive without the friction of constant questioning.

Addressing resistance begins with awareness rather than judgment. When you uncover a fear or limiting belief, acknowledge it without labeling it as failure. This mindset prevents the common trap of spiraling into self-criticism, which only deepens the block. Instead, explore the belief with curiosity: Where did it originate? Does it still serve you? Often, simply naming the fear reduces its grip because it is no longer operating unconsciously.

Releasing resistance can be supported through practices that calm the nervous system and reprogram the subconscious. Breathwork, journaling, and affirmations work synergistically when approached consistently. For example, writing out the fear followed by an empowering reframe — "I am safe to receive abundance," "Love supports me," "It is safe to be seen" — gradually conditions new patterns. Over time, these shifts create space for the manifestation to unfold without inner conflict.

Aligned action also needs refinement as circumstances evolve. Many people get stuck waiting for a sign to act, missing opportunities already available to them. Look for actions that feel expansive rather than forced. These may be small adjustments, like reaching out to a potential collaborator, committing to a healthier bedtime, or setting aside a portion of income for future goals. Each step affirms belief in the vision, even before external results appear.

A useful tool during periods of stagnation is regular self-inquiry. Ask yourself: "If my manifestation were guaranteed, how would I behave today?" This question bypasses doubt and guides decisions from the energy of already having, rather than the desperation of trying to get. Acting from this perspective rewires the subconscious to treat your desire as inevitable, accelerating its arrival.

Navigating timing requires both trust and discernment. There is a difference between a manifestation that is delayed because external pieces are still aligning and one that is blocked by internal patterns. Regular reflection helps clarify which is present. If you have addressed fears, taken aligned actions, and maintained openness, delays are often a matter of orchestration rather than error. In these moments, patience is not passive; it is an active state of staying receptive, continuing inner work, and preparing for the opportunity when it arrives.

Moments of apparent stillness can also be invitations to expand your vision. Sometimes what you are waiting for is smaller than what life intends to give you. The pause allows space for a desire to evolve — perhaps from wanting a specific job to seeking work that aligns with deeper purpose, or from envisioning a relationship to calling in partnership that supports your growth. This evolution often leads to outcomes richer than you first imagined.

Ultimately, stalls in manifestation are part of the process rather than signs of failure. They highlight where alignment is still forming and encourage a deeper relationship with trust, patience, and self-awareness. When you meet these pauses with curiosity instead of panic, you transform them into turning points. Instead of pushing harder, you soften into alignment — and that softening often becomes the very shift that unlocks everything.

Breaking Through Resistance and Self-Sabotage

Resistance and self-sabotage are not signs that you are failing at manifestation; they are signals pointing toward unprocessed fears and unhealed patterns. These behaviors often arise when you are close to growth, because receiving what you desire requires stepping beyond the familiar. The subconscious mind equates familiarity with safety, even if the familiar patterns are uncomfortable. Understanding this dynamic allows you to meet resistance with compassion rather than frustration and transform it into a pathway forward.

Recognizing the Forms of Resistance

Resistance is not always obvious. Sometimes it looks like procrastination or distraction, but it can also appear as overcomplication — constantly researching, planning, or waiting for perfect conditions instead of taking action. It might show up as chronic doubt, repeatedly questioning whether you are doing things "right" rather than trusting the process. These subtle behaviors drain energy and keep you looping in preparation rather than progress.

Self-sabotage often follows when resistance is left unexamined. This can look like abandoning routines just as momentum builds, pushing away opportunities that feel "too good," or engaging in habits that contradict stated goals. For instance, someone manifesting financial freedom might impulsively overspend when money finally arrives, unconsciously reinforcing a belief that they cannot handle abundance.

Tracing the Roots

At the core of both resistance and self-sabotage are protective mechanisms. The subconscious mind tries to shield you from perceived danger — failure, rejection, disappointment — by keeping you in known territory. Past experiences often program these patterns. A childhood memory of being criticized for mistakes might lead to perfectionism, while a past heartbreak could trigger avoidance whenever intimacy deepens.

Identifying these roots begins with self-inquiry. Ask yourself: "What do I fear will happen if I succeed?" The answers may surprise you. Many people discover fears around losing relationships, standing out, or being judged, rather than fear of failure itself. Naming these fears brings them into awareness, where they can be addressed instead of silently controlling behavior.

Shifting the Inner Dialogue

Breaking through resistance requires reframing how you relate to your inner critic. Harsh self-talk — "I always mess things up," "I'm just lazy" — reinforces the very patterns you want to release. Replacing these judgments with curiosity changes everything. When you notice procrastination, ask why your mind feels unsafe to move forward. What reassurance or resource would make progress feel manageable? This compassionate approach disarms resistance and opens space for new choices.

One effective way to dismantle self-sabotage is through incremental commitments. Large, sudden changes often trigger the subconscious to push back, interpreting them as unsafe. Smaller steps build familiarity and trust, allowing your nervous system to adjust gradually. For example, instead of committing to an hour of daily visualization, start with five minutes. Instead of aiming to save thousands at once, set aside a small but consistent amount. These micro-commitments accumulate and, over time, rewire your sense of what is normal and possible.

Creating supportive environments also reduces resistance. The spaces you inhabit either reinforce alignment or pull you into old patterns. Organize your surroundings so reminders of your vision are visible and distractions are minimized. This could mean decluttering, placing affirmations where you see them often, or designating a calm corner for reflection. Environment cues quietly signal safety and possibility, easing the subconscious fear of change.

Accountability can be another powerful tool when used intentionally. Sharing your goals with someone you trust — or even tracking progress privately — creates gentle external reinforcement without relying on pressure. The key is to pair accountability with compassion. When setbacks occur, instead of spiraling into shame, review what triggered the behavior and identify how to support yourself differently next time. This shift from punishment to learning transforms resistance into feedback rather than failure.

Inner trust grows as you consistently follow through on small promises to yourself. Each time you keep a commitment, no matter how minor, you prove to your subconscious that change is safe and sustainable. Over time, these repeated proofs dissolve the old narrative that you cannot be trusted to follow through, which is at the root of many self-sabotaging cycles.

It is equally important to celebrate progress along the way. Resistance thrives when you fixate on what is missing; acknowledging every step forward reinforces the identity of someone who moves through fear rather than being ruled by it. Whether it is completing a week of aligned habits or choosing a kinder response to yourself, recognizing these moments creates momentum that builds naturally over time.

Ultimately, breaking through resistance and self-sabotage is less about eradicating fear and more about building the capacity to act alongside it. Fear will still surface in new stages of growth, but your relationship to it changes. Instead of treating it as a stop sign, you learn to interpret it as a signal that expansion is happening. This mindset shift transforms obstacles into invitations — opportunities to integrate old lessons and rise into the version of yourself that can hold the manifestation you seek.

Using Feedback from "Delays" to Refine Your Alignment

Delays in manifestation can feel discouraging, especially when you have invested energy into clarity, belief, and consistent practice. Yet these pauses are rarely meaningless. They are feedback — signals offering information about where alignment can deepen or where adjustments may be needed. Interpreting delays through this lens transforms them from obstacles into opportunities for refinement. Rather than asking, "Why isn't it here yet?" the more powerful question becomes, "What is this teaching me about who I am becoming?"

Delays as Mirrors

Every desire you hold acts like a mirror, reflecting your current relationship to receiving. If your vision involves abundance, a delay may reveal lingering scarcity beliefs. If it involves love, a pause might highlight fears of intimacy or boundaries that need strengthening. The delay is not punishment; it is clarity. It shows where your current vibration and your desired reality are slightly misaligned.

Seeing delays as mirrors helps shift out of frustration and into curiosity. Instead of interpreting them as failure, you begin to approach them as part of the journey. This mindset prevents you from abandoning the process prematurely and opens the door to deeper self-awareness.

Identifying the Gaps

When manifestation feels stalled, consider whether the delay stems from internal misalignment, external timing, or a combination of both. Internal misalignment can look like conflicting beliefs, unaddressed fears, or actions that contradict your intentions. External timing often involves elements beyond your control, like opportunities or people aligning behind the scenes.

To discern which is present, reflect on your own energy. Are you consistently embodying the state you wish to create, or do you oscillate between belief and doubt? Do your daily actions reflect the reality you want, or are they reinforcing your current circumstances? This inquiry is not about blame but about gathering information. Once you identify the gaps, you can begin bridging them intentionally.

The Role of Emotional Feedback

Delays also provide emotional feedback. Persistent frustration, anxiety, or resentment around a manifestation often signals an attachment that blocks flow. When the desire feels heavy or desperate, the energy around it is constrictive rather than open. Recognizing this emotional state allows you to release pressure and return to trust.

Releasing attachment does not mean abandoning the desire. It means softening your grip on how and when it arrives. This openness creates space for solutions you might not have anticipated — and often allows manifestations to unfold in ways better than originally imagined.

One of the most powerful ways to engage with delays is through structured self-reflection. Ask questions that invite insight rather than criticism. What patterns keep resurfacing in your thoughts or behaviors? Are there emotions you have avoided processing that could be influencing your energy? Are there practical steps you have resisted because they feel uncomfortable or unfamiliar? Honest answers to these questions often reveal the subtle adjustments that unlock movement.

Reframing the concept of time itself can also transform your experience. Many people treat timelines as ultimatums, measuring their worth or the validity of the process by how quickly results appear. This mindset creates pressure that tightens energy and reinforces the very lack you are trying to transcend. Instead, view the timeline as fluid. The absence of visible results today does not mean nothing is happening; it simply means alignment is still unfolding behind the scenes. Holding this perspective allows you to remain steady rather than reactive.

During waiting periods, refining your alignment is less about doing more and more about deepening into being. Practices like mindfulness, gratitude, and visualization help anchor you in the present while still honoring your future vision. When you can genuinely appreciate where you are while holding faith in where you are headed, you dissolve resistance and create conditions for faster manifestation.

Practical alignment also means evaluating whether your actions reflect your desired reality. This is not about relentless striving but about congruence. If you are manifesting a healthier body, are you treating yourself with respect in daily routines? If you are calling in financial abundance, are you managing current resources with care? Each aligned choice becomes a vote for the reality you are creating, reinforcing belief and reducing inner conflict.

Delays often invite expansion beyond the original goal. A desire that once felt urgent might evolve into something richer or more aligned with your values. This is why flexibility is crucial; clinging to one fixed outcome can blind you to opportunities that are even better suited to your growth. By regularly revisiting your vision and asking, "Does this still resonate with who I am becoming?" you remain open to upgrades that exceed your initial imagination.

Finally, viewing delays as feedback builds resilience. Instead of spiraling into doubt each time progress slows, you learn to interpret pauses as checkpoints. They invite you to realign, recalibrate, and recommit with greater clarity. This mindset shift transforms the manifestation process from a series of anxieties into an unfolding journey — one where each step, visible or not, contributes to the ultimate outcome.

By approaching delays as guidance rather than punishment, you remain empowered even in stillness. This quiet confidence keeps you receptive to the subtle shifts and opportunities that signal alignment is deepening. Over time, the very delays that once felt frustrating become proof of your growth — and evidence that what you are calling in is preparing to arrive in its most aligned form.

Chapter 12: Living as the Receiver

How to Maintain Flow After Big Wins

Reaching a major milestone in manifestation can feel euphoric. The excitement, validation, and sense of possibility can be life-changing. Yet many people are surprised to find that after the initial high fades, old doubts or anxieties resurface. They fear losing what they have gained, or they stop doing the very practices that brought them success. Maintaining flow after big wins requires a shift from chasing goals to sustaining alignment — learning to live in a state of receiving rather than repeatedly starting over.

Why Post-Manifestation Plateaus Happen

Big wins trigger nervous system responses just as much as big challenges do. When you achieve something you once considered impossible, your subconscious may struggle to keep up with the new reality. This can lead to self-sabotage or subtle resistance, like second-guessing whether you "deserve" what you have received. It is not uncommon for people to unconsciously recreate old patterns after a win because those patterns feel familiar and therefore safe.

Understanding this helps remove shame from the experience. Feeling unsettled after success is not failure; it is your mind and body recalibrating to a higher level of possibility. Recognizing this adjustment period allows you to navigate it with awareness rather than panic.

Anchoring the New Normal

One of the most effective ways to sustain flow is to anchor the new reality as normal rather than exceptional. Celebrate your achievement, but also begin integrating it into your identity. Instead of seeing the win as a stroke of luck, affirm it as a reflection of who you are becoming. Ask yourself, "If this is now my baseline, how do I show up every day?" This mindset shift prevents the high from being temporary and helps build momentum for future growth.

Practices that reinforce this anchoring include visualization of the next chapter, gratitude for what has arrived, and continued alignment routines. It is tempting to relax these habits after reaching a goal, but they are what stabilize your energy and keep you receptive. The point is not to cling to the manifestation but to nurture the version of you capable of holding it with ease.

Navigating the Fear of Loss

Success often brings unexpected fears — fear of losing what you have gained, fear of judgment from others, or fear of not being able to repeat the result. These fears are natural, but left unchecked, they can close the very flow that allowed the manifestation to occur. The antidote is trust. Trust that what is aligned cannot be taken from you, and that even if circumstances shift, you have the capacity to create again.

Building this trust requires staying connected to the inner practices that carried you to this point. Reflection, emotional regulation, and conscious gratitude remind you that abundance is not a one-time event but an ongoing relationship. By treating success as an invitation to deepen alignment rather than a finish line, you prevent the cycle of expansion and contraction that keeps many people stuck at the same level.

Big wins can serve as launchpads if approached with curiosity rather than complacency. Instead of focusing on replicating the exact conditions that led to success, reflect on the deeper principles that supported it. Was it consistency? Emotional regulation? Trust in timing? Identifying these core elements allows you to apply them to new goals without becoming rigid or superstitious about specific routines. This flexibility keeps your manifestation practice alive rather than mechanical.

A key aspect of maintaining flow is humility balanced with self-acknowledgment. It is important to celebrate how far you have come without slipping into the belief that you have "arrived" or no longer need growth. Humility keeps you open to learning, while acknowledgment prevents you from downplaying your accomplishments. Together, they create a steady state where gratitude and ambition coexist harmoniously.

Energy hygiene becomes more essential after major breakthroughs. Greater visibility or responsibility often accompanies big wins, which can expose you to new pressures or external projections. Establishing practices that keep your energy clear — such as regular solitude, journaling, or mindful movement — ensures you remain grounded in your own alignment rather than pulled into other people's expectations. This grounding is what allows you to continue manifesting from authenticity rather than reaction.

Another common challenge after success is the subtle pressure to constantly outdo yourself. The mind may frame growth as a series of escalating milestones, where each win must be bigger than the last. This mindset creates exhaustion and erodes the joy of the process. Reframing growth as depth rather than constant expansion shifts the focus to quality over quantity — cultivating richer experiences, deeper relationships, and more meaningful goals rather than chasing endless metrics of "more."

To sustain flow, it is helpful to redefine success not as a single event but as a way of being. This involves asking different questions: not "What can I manifest next?" but "Who am I becoming as I manifest?" This perspective transforms manifestation from a results-oriented practice into a lifelong path of alignment and self-mastery. Big wins then become milestones along the way rather than destinations, and your sense of fulfillment remains steady regardless of external fluctuations.

The final piece of maintaining flow lies in gratitude that evolves. Initial gratitude often focuses on the arrival of what you desired. Sustained gratitude, however, expands to encompass the entire journey — the lessons learned, the resilience built, the moments of doubt that refined your trust. This broader gratitude not only stabilizes the energy around your current manifestations but also magnetizes future ones, as it signals to your subconscious and to life itself that you are ready to hold more with appreciation rather than fear.

When you treat big wins as invitations to deepen alignment, they stop being fleeting highs and become foundations for sustained growth. You carry forward the energy that created them, allowing each success to compound into the next stage of your evolution. Rather than fearing that the flow will end, you learn to live within it — and from that space, manifestation becomes less about single outcomes and more about the life you continuously create.

Becoming the Version of You Who Always Receives

True manifestation is not about singular victories but about embodying a state where receiving becomes natural. Many people approach manifestation as a series of isolated events — visualizing one goal, celebrating its arrival, and then starting over. This cycle often overlooks the deeper transformation required to sustain abundance. To consistently receive, you must shift identity at its core, becoming someone for whom alignment and openness are not temporary states but a way of being.

Identity and Manifestation

Your identity shapes what you believe is possible and, by extension, what you allow yourself to experience. If you see yourself as someone who struggles, who always has to work twice as hard, or who is perpetually overlooked, your actions and energy unconsciously reinforce that narrative. Conversely, when you begin to view yourself as capable of ease, worthy of abundance, and open to support, you align with opportunities that reflect those beliefs.

This is not about pretending or forcing false positivity. It is about expanding your self-concept to include what you desire. Ask yourself: "Who would I be if receiving were natural? How would I think, speak, and act?" The answers to these questions reveal the qualities you need to cultivate — confidence, trust, gratitude — so that receiving becomes an extension of your identity rather than an exception to it.

Releasing the Struggle Narrative

Many people carry unconscious loyalty to struggle. They have been conditioned to believe that worthiness must be earned through constant effort or sacrifice. This belief leads them to reject ease, even when it is available. Opportunities might arise, but they feel undeserved or unsafe, prompting self-sabotage. Recognizing this pattern is essential. It allows you to replace the narrative of "I must fight for everything" with "I am worthy of receiving without suffering first."

This shift does not remove the need for action but changes the energy behind it. You continue to take steps toward your goals, but those steps flow from desire and alignment rather than fear or scarcity. Over time, this change in motivation alters both the pace and quality of your manifestations.

Embodying Receptive Energy

Receiving is an active state, not a passive one. It requires openness, presence, and trust. A receptive person notices opportunities rather than overlooking them, acts on intuition rather than dismissing it, and expresses gratitude even for small signs of progress. Cultivating this energy involves regulating the nervous system so it feels safe to hold more — more love, more money, more recognition.

Simple practices like mindful breathing, body awareness, or gratitude journaling help anchor receptivity. These habits remind the mind and body that expansion does not equal danger. As safety grows, so does your capacity to receive without tension or fear of loss.

Integrating this receptive identity into daily life begins with the smallest choices. Every decision — from how you speak to yourself in quiet moments to how you respond when opportunities appear — reinforces either the old self or the emerging one. When you choose thoughts and actions that align with the person you are becoming, even if they feel unfamiliar, you are training your subconscious to normalize receiving. Over time, this repeated alignment builds an internal consistency that makes abundance feel inevitable rather than extraordinary.

Maintaining this identity also involves staying grounded during inevitable fluctuations. Life will still bring challenges, but how you interpret them changes. Instead of seeing difficulties as evidence that manifestation has failed, you recognize them as opportunities to deepen trust and refine focus. This mindset prevents you from collapsing back into scarcity at the first sign of resistance. It allows you to hold the bigger picture, knowing that setbacks do not erase progress but often precede breakthroughs.

A vital part of sustaining a receiving identity is tending to your internal dialogue. Even after significant growth, remnants of old narratives may surface — thoughts like "this is too good to last" or "I am not ready for this level." Rather than suppressing these doubts, meet them with gentle curiosity. Question their validity and replace them with statements that reflect your chosen reality, such as "I am capable of sustaining what I attract" or "Good things are safe to receive." This ongoing reconditioning ensures that moments of fear become catalysts for deeper embodiment rather than obstacles.

As your capacity to receive expands, so does your ability to give. True abundance naturally flows outward; the more secure you feel in what you have, the more willing you become to share. This does not always mean material giving — it can manifest as generosity of time, encouragement, or presence. When receiving and giving exist in balance, you step into a cycle of circulation rather than hoarding, which keeps energy flowing and prevents stagnation.

The most profound shift occurs when receiving becomes less about isolated manifestations and more about living in a state of alignment. You are no longer measuring your worth by individual achievements but by the harmony between your inner world and the life unfolding around you. From this place, even desires evolve. They become less about proving something and more about expressing your deepest values and potential. Manifestation stops being a means to an end and becomes an ongoing dialogue with life itself.

When you live as the version of yourself who always receives, you release the constant striving that once defined your pursuit of goals. You step into ease, where desires emerge and unfold naturally without forcing. This is not complacency but mastery — the quiet confidence of knowing you are supported, aligned, and capable of co-creating with life at every level. It is this state, more than any single technique or ritual, that transforms manifestation from a practice into a way of being.

Expanding Beyond Personal Goals into Purpose and Service

Manifestation often begins with personal desires — financial freedom, fulfilling relationships, better health. These goals are powerful entry points because they motivate action and invite you to explore your beliefs about what is possible. Yet there is a point in every journey where personal achievement alone stops feeling complete. You reach a level of fulfillment that calls you to something larger: aligning your manifestations with purpose and service. This shift does not diminish personal desires; it integrates them into a broader vision that sustains deeper meaning.

The Evolution of Desire

Personal goals tend to answer the question "What do I want?" Purpose reframes it into "How can what I create contribute?" This evolution happens naturally as you grow. Once your basic needs are met and you experience the joy of receiving, you begin to notice a desire to share, uplift, or impact others. It is not about abandoning your own dreams but about expanding them so they create ripples beyond yourself.

This transition reflects a deeper truth about abundance: it flows more freely when it circulates. When your manifestations serve not only you but others, they gain momentum. The energy behind them becomes expansive rather than insular, tapping into a current of purpose that naturally attracts greater opportunities and support.

Finding Alignment Between Personal Joy and Collective Impact

Purpose is often misunderstood as something self-sacrificing, as though serving others means denying your own happiness. In reality, authentic purpose is found where personal joy and collective impact intersect. It is about identifying what lights you up and exploring how that passion can create value beyond your own life. A musician may feel this when their art inspires others, or an entrepreneur when their innovation solves a problem that matters to them personally.

This approach prevents burnout because it honors both your needs and the needs of others. It allows manifestation to feel sustainable rather than depleting, since you are creating from a place of genuine enthusiasm rather than obligation.

From Success to Significance

Shifting into purpose invites a broader definition of success. Achievements that once seemed monumental become stepping stones toward something more enduring: significance. Significance is not measured solely by wealth or recognition but by the positive change your life generates. This might manifest as raising a family in a loving environment, mentoring others on their path, or creating work that continues to inspire long after you are gone. Discovering purpose often begins with noticing where your natural gifts meet the needs of others. Pay attention to the moments when helping someone else feels effortless and energizing rather than draining. These experiences reveal where your personal strengths intersect with a desire to contribute. Purpose is rarely found by forcing yourself into a role you think you "should" play; it emerges when you honor what feels most alive in you and explore how it can uplift others.

Service rooted in authenticity also reshapes how you approach manifestation. Instead of asking only how a desire will benefit you, begin considering who else it might impact. A financial goal may become a vehicle for supporting loved ones or funding meaningful projects. A personal achievement might inspire others to believe in what is possible for them. This perspective transforms goals into channels for collective good without sacrificing personal joy.

Integrating service into your manifestations requires balance. It is not about neglecting yourself or overextending to please others. True service flows from overflow — the surplus energy and abundance you generate by tending to your own alignment first. When you are nourished, giving becomes effortless rather than obligatory. From this state, your impact is sustainable and free of resentment because it arises from genuine desire rather than pressure.

Living with purpose also invites you to think long-term. Personal goals often center on immediate milestones, while purpose looks at legacy. How will the choices you make today shape the lives of others tomorrow? This shift encourages patience and perspective, helping you navigate challenges with resilience. Obstacles become part of a larger story rather than isolated setbacks, and your sense of fulfillment grows deeper because you see the ripples of your actions over time.

The greatest reward of expanding into purpose and service is the alignment it creates with life itself. You begin to feel supported by something larger than your own willpower, as though the universe meets you halfway when your intentions benefit more than just you. Opportunities appear not because you are forcing them, but because your energy is harmonizing with a broader flow. In this state, manifestation becomes less about acquiring and more about expressing — an ongoing dance of giving and receiving that continually enriches you and those around you.

When personal goals evolve into purpose, you step into a form of abundance that cannot be measured solely in material terms. There is a quiet satisfaction in knowing that what you create matters beyond the moment. This sense of contribution fuels ongoing growth and makes each manifestation feel like part of a greater tapestry rather than a standalone achievement. It is here that manifestation transcends technique and becomes a way of living — not just for yourself, but for something far bigger.

Conclusion: The New Way Forward

Your Transformation Isn't an Event, It's a Way of Being

Transformation is often imagined as a single defining moment — a breakthrough that changes everything overnight. While powerful insights and pivotal experiences can occur, lasting change rarely hinges on one event. True transformation is cultivated over time, through choices repeated daily, beliefs steadily reprogrammed, and a deepening relationship with your own inner world. It is less about a finish line and more about living in a new state of alignment, one that continually evolves as you do.

Why the "Event" Mentality Falls Short

The idea of transformation as an event can create unnecessary pressure. People wait for the perfect seminar, book, or spiritual awakening that will instantly solve their struggles. This expectation leads to cycles of disappointment because external moments, while inspiring, cannot replace the inner work of integration. Without consistent application, even the most profound realization fades back into old patterns.

Approaching transformation as a way of being shifts the focus from waiting to embodying. Instead of asking, "When will I finally get there?" the question becomes, "How can I live this truth now?" This perspective empowers you to take ownership of your growth rather than outsourcing it to circumstances or timing.

Living in Alignment

A way-of-being transformation is rooted in alignment — the congruence between what you believe, how you feel, and the actions you take. This alignment is dynamic, not rigid. It allows for growth, mistakes, and recalibration without losing sight of your core values. Living in alignment does not mean perfection; it means continually returning to center, even when life pulls you in different directions.

In practical terms, this looks like embodying your desired state long before results arrive. If you are manifesting abundance, you practice gratitude and wise stewardship with what you already have. If you seek love, you nurture self-respect and connection in your daily interactions. These choices gradually reshape your identity until receiving what you desire feels natural rather than exceptional.

The Role of Consistency

Small, consistent practices create lasting change more effectively than sporadic bursts of effort. A single meditation may offer clarity, but a daily practice rewires your nervous system. One journal entry can inspire insight, but ongoing reflection reveals patterns and breakthroughs that transform how you navigate life.

Consistency builds trust within yourself. Each time you follow through on a commitment — whether it is maintaining a ritual, speaking kindly to yourself, or honoring your boundaries — you reinforce the belief that change is possible and sustainable. This inner trust becomes the foundation for deeper manifestations, because you no longer doubt your ability to hold what you call in.

As transformation deepens, the way you relate to goals evolves. Instead of chasing outcomes as proof of worth or validation, you begin to see them as milestones in an ongoing journey. Achieving a goal becomes less about relief and more about confirmation that your alignment is working. This perspective allows you to release the constant tension of striving and to enjoy the process itself. Goals stop being an escape from your current life and become expressions of who you already are.

This shift also changes your understanding of success. Traditional success is often measured by external markers: income, status, possessions. While these can still hold value, a way-of-being transformation prioritizes inner markers such as peace, integrity, and fulfillment. You notice the subtle ways your life feels lighter, how challenges no longer trigger the same reactions, and how gratitude arises naturally. These internal signs are just as important as visible achievements, because they indicate the foundation on which lasting manifestations are built.

Sustaining this transformation requires ongoing presence. It is easy to slip into autopilot once life improves, forgetting the practices that created the change. Presence keeps you aware of where you stand, what thoughts you entertain, and how your energy feels. It helps you catch subtle misalignments early, before they grow into major detours. This is not about hyper-vigilance but about cultivating a gentle awareness that becomes second nature over time.

A vital component of this new way of being is compassion toward yourself. Even with growth, you will encounter moments of resistance, fear, or old habits resurfacing. Compassion allows you to meet these moments without judgment, which prevents spiraling into shame or self-criticism. Instead of interpreting setbacks as failure, you see them as opportunities to practice the very alignment you are embodying. Compassion is what keeps the transformation sustainable rather than exhausting.

Living in this state also invites expansion beyond personal gain. When you feel secure in your own alignment, you naturally begin to consider how your growth can benefit others. This does not mean taking on responsibility for everyone around you but recognizing that your presence influences those you encounter. The calm you cultivate ripples outward; your ability to navigate challenges becomes a quiet example for others still searching for their path.

Ultimately, this ongoing transformation is about becoming the clearest expression of yourself. It is not a fixed destination but a continual unfolding, where each step reveals more of what is possible. There is no finish line to cross, only deeper levels of alignment to explore. When you embrace this, manifestation stops being something you do and becomes who you are — a natural flow of intention, trust, and inspired action that shapes every area of life.

This way of being frees you from the cycle of highs and lows that once defined personal growth. You are no longer waiting for a single breakthrough to change everything; you are living the breakthrough every day. And from this steady foundation, everything you desire — and more than you imagined possible — begins to arrive with ease.

How to Keep Growing and Manifesting Bigger with Less Effort

As your practice matures, a natural question arises: how do you continue to expand without returning to the exhausting patterns of constant striving? At first, manifestation can feel like an intensive effort — consistent journaling, visualization, affirmations, and emotional recalibration. These practices are vital for building a foundation, but over time, they are meant to evolve. True mastery is not about doing more; it is about embodying more. Growth becomes about subtle shifts in awareness rather than forceful effort.

The Principle of Effortless Expansion

Effortless expansion is not the absence of action but the absence of unnecessary resistance. In the early stages of manifestation, much of your energy goes toward dismantling limiting beliefs and proving to yourself that change is possible. Once this groundwork is complete, you no longer need to convince yourself; you simply act from alignment. This reduces friction and allows growth to feel lighter and faster, even as the manifestations themselves become bigger.

The paradox of expansion is that the more you trust the process, the less you need to control it. Trust frees mental and emotional bandwidth that was previously consumed by doubt or hyper-vigilance. This energy can now be directed toward inspired actions that accelerate results rather than scattered efforts that dilute them.

Expanding Your Capacity to Receive

To manifest bigger with less effort, you must also expand your capacity to receive. Larger manifestations require holding more energy — more abundance, more responsibility, more visibility. If your nervous system interprets this expansion as unsafe, it will unconsciously sabotage progress to return to familiar ground. Preparing for bigger manifestations means gradually increasing your comfort with holding more.

This can be cultivated through practices that strengthen emotional resilience and groundedness. Mindfulness, breathwork, and even celebrating small wins train your body to normalize higher levels of abundance. As your internal threshold rises, what once felt overwhelming becomes manageable, and your external reality mirrors this shift.

Shifting from Doing to Being

The most profound growth occurs when you transition from "doing manifestation" to "being manifesting." Instead of rigidly following techniques, you naturally embody the energy of what you desire. Gratitude, trust, and alignment become habitual, woven into your daily life rather than reserved for special rituals. This does not mean abandoning practices altogether but allowing them to evolve. A morning routine may shift from intensive scripting to a few quiet moments of connection. Visualization may happen spontaneously throughout the day rather than in structured sessions.

When being replaces constant doing, growth accelerates because every moment reinforces alignment. Life itself becomes the practice, and even ordinary experiences — a conversation, a walk, a pause to breathe — become opportunities to embody the version of you who is already receiving.

Maintaining effortless expansion over time depends on your willingness to evolve with your manifestations. Each new level brings unique challenges and opportunities for refinement. The practices that served you at one stage may need to be simplified or deepened at another. Instead of rigidly holding onto old methods, allow yourself to adapt. Flexibility keeps manifestation alive and prevents it from becoming another form of control disguised as spirituality.

Scaling desires without losing alignment requires clarity around why you want them. Bigger goals can easily activate old patterns of scarcity if pursued from ego or comparison. When desires are rooted in genuine joy and aligned with your values, they grow without destabilizing you. Asking yourself whether a bigger vision feels expansive or heavy helps ensure you are chasing resonance rather than status. This self-inquiry prevents burnout and keeps growth connected to meaning rather than performance.

Fulfillment is also sustained by continuing to nurture the foundation you have built. Even as goals become larger, the principles remain the same: gratitude, presence, trust, and inspired action. These are not just entry-level practices; they are the pillars that support every stage of expansion.

Neglecting them in favor of chasing new techniques often leads to imbalance. Returning to these fundamentals grounds you, no matter how ambitious your vision becomes.

An overlooked aspect of manifesting bigger with less effort is creating space for integration. Rapid growth can feel exhilarating but also destabilizing if you do not pause to absorb it. Integration allows your identity to catch up with your reality, preventing the subtle self-sabotage that arises when success feels unfamiliar. Making time to celebrate wins, reflect on lessons, and adjust your vision ensures that expansion remains sustainable rather than overwhelming.

Over time, effortless manifestation becomes less about "attracting" and more about "allowing." You stop treating desires as things you must pull toward you and begin seeing them as natural extensions of who you are. This shift dissolves urgency and invites a deeper sense of peace. Manifestation stops feeling like a test to pass and starts feeling like a partnership with life, where you trust timing and remain open to surprises that exceed your expectations.

The more you live in this state, the more you notice that growth is no longer linear. It unfolds in waves, with periods of rapid expansion followed by quieter seasons of integration. Instead of resisting these rhythms, you learn to work with them. You use slower periods to rest, refine, and prepare for the next surge. This cyclical approach keeps growth balanced and ensures that each level of manifestation builds on a stable foundation rather than crumbling under pressure.

When you understand that bigger manifestations require less effort, not more, you free yourself from the exhausting chase for "next." You live in alignment now, and that alignment naturally scales as your vision expands. The energy you once poured into forcing outcomes is redirected into living fully — enjoying, contributing, and continuously growing without needing to prove anything. From this place, your manifestations do not just increase in size; they deepen in meaning, becoming reflections of a life fully aligned with who you truly are.

Next Steps to Integrate This Work into Every Aspect of Your Life

The most significant shift you can make now is to stop seeing manifestation as something you do occasionally and start living it as a natural extension of who you are. Integration is where theory becomes experience. It is the moment you bridge what you have learned with how you move through the world — how you think, feel, and respond to daily life. This step is not about perfection but about consistency, layering small choices that steadily transform your identity.

Bringing Alignment Into the Everyday

Many people compartmentalize their growth. They meditate in the morning, visualize at night, but spend the rest of the day unconsciously reacting to circumstances. Integration dissolves these walls. It invites you to carry alignment into every interaction — at work, with family, in moments of solitude. Manifestation stops being something that happens during rituals and becomes the lens through which you see the world.

This means noticing your energy in real time rather than only during dedicated practices. When you catch yourself slipping into worry or comparison, you gently guide your thoughts back to trust. When opportunities arise, you listen to intuition instead of defaulting to fear. These micro-adjustments are where long-term transformation takes root, because they prove that alignment is possible even in the middle of real life.

Anchoring Identity Through Repetition

Lasting change requires repetition, but not in the rigid sense of forcing daily routines. It is about consistently choosing thoughts, emotions, and actions that align with the version of you who already lives what you desire. Each aligned choice rewires your subconscious, gradually replacing old narratives with new truths. This process is subtle yet powerful, often unfolding without dramatic fanfare.

Simple anchors — gratitude upon waking, intentional breathing before big decisions, reflection at the end of the day — reinforce alignment without overwhelming your schedule. These practices work because they integrate seamlessly into life rather than demanding extra time or creating pressure to perform them perfectly. Integration succeeds when it feels natural, not forced.

Preparing for the Shifts Ahead

As you embody this work, expect your external reality to shift. Relationships may change, opportunities may appear, and old patterns may fall away. Some changes will feel exhilarating; others may feel disorienting. Both are signs of growth. The more grounded you are in your practices, the more gracefully you navigate these transitions.

Integration also calls for discernment. Not every impulse is aligned action, and not every challenge is resistance to push through. Part of mastery is learning to pause, check in with your values, and respond rather than react. This intentionality ensures that your manifestations expand your life in meaningful ways rather than simply adding more noise.

Sustaining alignment long term requires creating a rhythm that grows with you. Early in your journey, structure helps establish the foundation — regular journaling, dedicated time for visualization, clear routines for gratitude and reflection. As those habits become second nature, they evolve into a fluid practice woven into daily living. The goal is not to cling to rituals but to use them as touchstones that keep you connected, even as life circumstances change.

The most effective way to ensure this work endures is to treat it as an ongoing dialogue rather than a fixed program. Continue asking yourself questions that expand your awareness: How am I feeling in this moment? Where am I acting from trust versus fear? Which desires still excite me, and which no longer feel aligned? This kind of self-inquiry keeps your path alive and prevents you from stagnating in outdated goals or practices.

Another key aspect of integration is allowing your vision to evolve. What you desire today may transform as you grow. Clinging to old dreams can create friction if they no longer reflect who you are becoming. By staying open, you allow manifestations to match your current frequency rather than outdated expectations. This openness also invites outcomes beyond what you originally imagined, often leading to experiences richer than your initial vision.

Support is equally important in sustaining integration. Surrounding yourself with environments and relationships that reinforce your growth helps stabilize new patterns. This does not necessarily mean removing everyone who does not share your beliefs but rather creating a balance where your energy is protected and nourished. Supportive communities, mentors, or even a single accountability partner can provide perspective and encouragement during inevitable periods of doubt or transition.

Integration also involves recognizing when to rest. Growth is not constant acceleration; it includes seasons of quiet where assimilation occurs beneath the surface. Honoring these pauses prevents burnout and allows deeper embodiment. It is during these quieter phases that insights settle, new identities root, and the groundwork for the next phase of expansion forms. Finally, the deepest integration occurs when manifestation stops feeling like something separate from your life and becomes the natural expression of how you live. Every decision, every interaction, every response becomes an opportunity to align with your highest self. This is where the work transcends techniques and becomes who you are. From this place, growth continues effortlessly, and each new level of manifestation feels like an organic unfolding rather than a battle to be won.

When you reach this state, there is no finish line to cross, no singular moment of arrival. There is only continuous evolution, grounded in trust and expanded by curiosity. The next step is always simply the next aligned step — a quiet, steady commitment to living as the fullest version of yourself in every area of life. Over time, this way of being not only transforms what you receive but also deepens how you give, creating a cycle of abundance that sustains itself.

www.ingramcontent.com/pod-product-compliance
Lightning Source LLC
Chambersburg PA
CBHW050643160426
43194CB00010B/1788